Balancing Act

Australia Between Recession And Renewal

George Megalogenis

16

EasyRead Large

RHYW

Copyright Page from the Original Book

Published by Black Inc.,
an imprint of Schwartz Publishing Pty Ltd
Level 1, 221 Drummond Street
Carlton VIC 3053, Australia
enquiries@blackincbooks.com
www.blackincbooks.com

"Balancing Act" previously published as Quarterly Essay 61.
"Afterword" previously published as "Australia Divided" in the *Monthly*, December 2016–January 2017. "Trivial Pursuit" previously published as Quarterly Essay 40.

This revised edition published 2017.

National Library of Australia Cataloguing-in-Publication entry:
Megalogenis, George, author.
Balancing act: Australia between recession and renewal / George Megalogenis.
9781863959087 (paperback)
9781925435511 (ebook)
Politics, Practical–Australia.
Recessions–Australia.
Capitalism–Social aspects–Australia.
Social change–Australia.
Monetary policy–Australia.
Australia–Economic policy–21st century.
Australia–Economic conditions–21st century.
Australia–Politics and government–21st century.

Cover design by Peter Long
Text design and typesetting by Tristan Main

Printed in Australia by McPherson's Printing Group.

TABLE OF CONTENTS

BALANCING ACT

Australia Between Recession and Renewal

Introduction

Australia is in transition. Saying it is easy. The panic kicks in when we are compelled to describe what the future might look like. There is no complacent middle to aim at. We will either catch the next wave of prosperity, or finally succumb to the Great Recession.

Each force that is pulling apart our present reads like a turgid unit in a university degree. The technological revolution. Population ageing. The Asian century. Global warming. The mining boom, and bust. The crisis in capitalism. What are the challenges and opportunities? Discuss.

Some of our leaders have revelled in the detail. Kevin Rudd wanted to be across every subject, although he couldn't stick to any one topic long enough for the public to catch up. The annoying imprecision of his method sent his successors to the other extreme of simplicity. It will be impossible for coming generations to separate the banalities of Julia Gillard from those of Tony Abbott. "Moving forward" and "Stop the boats" will be slogans shorn of their contexts, and our children will wonder if our prime ministers were really that shallow. No, they were the most talented politicians of their era, their old supporters will reply. It was just that governing was impossible in the digital age.

Malcolm Turnbull brings us back to where we started with Kevin07 – this is a leader who professes to be unafraid of the future. But we are no closer to understanding where the world is heading, or our place in it. We do know we want to remain affluent and egalitarian. Turnbull had that platitude worked out before he took over. He told us on the day he sought the Liberal leadership in September 2015 that he wants Australia "to remain a high-wage, generous social-welfare net, first-world society." But in making that pledge, he acknowledged the root of our anxiety: the fear that we will be overrun by globalisation once China no longer has any need for our coal and iron ore.

The national mood has been defensive for so many years now that it is hard to recall the last time we were genuinely free of hang-ups and could look to the future with optimism. We greeted the new millennium as the cheery hosts of the Sydney Olympics, but virtually every message we have sent to the world since then has betrayed our parochialism. The *Tampa* episode of 2001 marked the birth of a long, complex phase of Australian insularity. Its first peak had nothing to do with asylum seekers. It came a few years after the *Tampa,* when the boats had stopped and the mining boom was underway. John Howard gave back every windfall dollar in the budget so that we could treat ourselves. That was the more revealing expression of our self-absorption, unprompted by a global crisis. We simply didn't care enough about the future to reinvest some of that money on behalf of our children. But then Howard double-crossed voters with his WorkChoices program, and the true source of our anger was confirmed – it was globalisation itself. With WorkChoices, Howard reminded Australians that their government no longer felt obliged to defend them against the open economy. Rudd's election win in 2007 briefly broke the spell. We applauded his handling of the global financial crisis, but once the danger had passed he lost his governing nerve, and a new cycle of narcissism commenced. The boats returned in 2009, reviving the old Australian dread of foreign invasion. Abbott ultimately turned the asylum seekers back again with the help of Labor's more punitive policies, but still we were miserable, with him in particular and the world in general.

The supposed strengths of the Australian character – our openness, our love of technology, our pluck – have been notably absent in our attitude to the future. Put bluntly, we don't have a plan. We know we need one, written jointly across government, business, trade unions and civil society. But we keep finding excuses to return to the trenches of our prejudice. Even there, within the sanctuary of the tribe, there is little cohesion. The Liberal Party is split along fault-lines of ideology and personality. Labor still lacks purpose. The trade unions divide between the ineffective and the corrupt. Within my own profession, the media, too many commentators have assigned themselves to covering their rivals. News Corp, for instance, deploys more resources to attacking the ABC than analysing the economy. Only business appears to have unity of purpose in its relentless pursuit of concessions from government.

The most consistent message sent by voters to the main parties over the past decade and a half has been the demand for security. Both sides have taken this to mean border protection and bribes at the ballot box; one fist clenched against the rest of the world, while the other hand offers cash to the most aggrieved. Yet each leader that tried this was bewildered when voters could not be appeased. The truth is that the demand for security is more sophisticated than politics has allowed. We want our leaders to think for the long term; to prepare us for life beyond the mining boom. Both sides have found this in their research since the earliest days of the boom, but both have been unable to see past the next Newspoll. Something deeper is happening here than the predictable incompetence of politics. The system knows what voters are really asking for: a return to some form of government intervention in the economy. Yet this is resisted because of a misguided faith in the open economic model. The only leader who seriously tried to find a way out of the impasse was Rudd, but he lost focus after the global financial crisis. Now a Liberal prime minister is being asked by the public to redraw the line between the market and the state.

The economy was the primary reason Turnbull gave for challenging Abbott. "It is clear enough that the government is not successful in providing the economic leadership that we need," he declared.

> It is not the fault of individual ministers. Ultimately the prime minister has not been capable of providing the economic leadership our nation needs; he has not been capable of providing the economic confidence that business needs ... The big economic changes that we're living through here and around the world offer enormous challenges and enormous opportunities and we need a different style of leadership. We need a style of leadership that ... explains the challenges and how to seize the opportunities. A style of leadership that respects the people's intelligence ... We need advocacy, not slogans.

***

He wasn't pitching to undecided colleagues, because the numbers to topple Abbott were already locked in. This assessment was delivered for the benefit of the public, and even now it remains the most remarkable admission that a Coalition government has made while in office.

No previous regime removed its leader on grounds of economic incompetence, although others probably should have. Before Abbott, the conservatives had replaced three sitting prime ministers – Billy Hughes in 1923, Robert Menzies in 1941 and John Gorton in 1971. In each case, the basic complaint was leadership style: arrogance, in short.

With Abbott, the personal and the polling were secondary to economic management. His erratic, uninspiring leadership demoralised business and consumers to an extent that no prime minister had since Gough Whitlam. Confidence in the future is the essential ingredient of economic growth. For a nation in transition, a loss of confidence can create a self-fulfilling prophecy of missed opportunities. Businesses become risk-averse. Consumers close their wallets. Employers respond to that weaker demand by cutting costs. Workers react to the squeeze on their wages by reducing spending. And so on, until growth stalls.

It was on Abbott's watch that we finally lost our global economic bragging right. The verdict was confirmed on the very day he was ousted, 14 September 2015, when the International Monetary Fund released its annual review of the Australian economy. "Australia has enjoyed exceptionally strong income growth for the past two decades," the IMF concluded. "But the waning resource investment boom and sharp fall in the terms of trade have brought this to a halt. A cyclical recovery is likely in the near term, but over the medium term, income growth is likely to slow to a rate in line with other advanced economies."

Identifying when Australia's long run of economic over-achievement ended is relatively easy. It was June 2014, when our unemployment rate crossed 6 per cent for the first time in eleven years. Timing matters here. This was just one month after the release of the Abbott government's pugnacious first budget. Unemployment had been creeping up in the final year of the Rudd–Gillard government. The economy needed support. But the new regime was screaming "budget emergency" and even though the Senate blocked the most contentious cuts, the announcement alone was sufficient to push unemployment over the 6 per cent threshold. The unusual part of this story is that unemployment rose despite the recovery in the United States. This had never happened before. The Australian and American unemployment rates had moved in the same direction, up or down, since at least the 1940s, reflecting the gravitational pull of the world's largest economy. That connection held throughout the mining boom, and even in the Great Recession itself. A revival in the United States should have lifted activity in Australia, but this time it didn't.

The media post-mortems did consider the role that the 2014 budget played in Abbott's removal, but very little attention was given to the damage it did to the economy. "The defining economic event of the government's life was its first budget," Peter Hartcher wrote in a five-part series of articles for the Fairfax newspapers. "[It] 'brought the government to the brink of destruction' as Abbott later conceded privately."

> From the time that budget was delivered, the Abbott government was fated to never again lead in the polls. It was overreach on a monumental scale and broke all the rules of political management – the government broke promises, had no mandate, failed to prepare public opinion, and misjudged the Senate and public opinion so profoundly that most of its hallmark measures became moribund, at a dead end in the Senate.

***

This is where the analysis stopped: at the marketing. The article was not designed to assess the individual measures; it was a news feature, not an economic think-piece. But it was typical of the weight the media placed on the personal and political when cataloguing the many disappointments of the Abbott government. (To be fair, journalists had an embarrassment of anecdotes to distract them.)

This focus on the personal and political meant that a discredited government had the final word on the question of economic competence. Abbott and his supporters were free to maintain the illusion that the policies blocked by the Senate were in the national interest. They would only plead guilty to the lesser crime of poor salesmanship. Joe Hockey, the treasurer who failed to pass that first budget, used his farewell speech to parliament to chide everyone but himself. "Mr Speaker, the Abbott government was good at policy but struggled with politics ... I admit that we could have done more to win over third-party endorsements and to win over the Senate; and we could have done more to win over the Australian people." It was a Clayton's contrition. He concluded this section of his valedictory by asserting that "the government had more courage than the parliament."

Hockey had the humility to depart politics. Abbott remained, extending his festival of self-pity into an election year and beyond. In defending his record, Abbott claimed to be supporting Turnbull's government. Not even Rudd was this crass. And so the question of competence which Turnbull raised is yet to be addressed.

Our political history offers little comfort to Turnbull, because the governments which transformed the economy in the past were Labor, not conservative. The first was led by John Curtin, the second by Bob Hawke. Both had treasurers who were their equal, and who succeeded them as prime minister. In each case, Labor had consciously changed its governing culture in response to a global catastrophe. The key members of the Curtin–Chifley government lived through the collapse of Jim Scullin's Labor government during the darkest years of the Great Depression. The Hawke–Keating ministry witnessed the implosion of Gough Whitlam's government. On both occasions,

Labor remade itself in Opposition before it returned to power.

To inspire a similar transformation in a Coalition government, Turnbull had to convince his colleagues they had already failed in office. They couldn't pretend that their former leader was an anomaly – a poor communicator with a brilliant program – because it was the conservative agenda for small government which undermined confidence.

Labor and now Liberal have made the same inexcusable blunder. They took the shortcut to power without the necessary policy renewal in Opposition. When they found governing much harder than expected, they turned to what they knew best – politics – and removed a first-term prime minister. Policy renewal could wait until after they had secured re-election with a new leader. The question for Turnbull is whether he can buy enough time to reset the system. One three-year term surely won't be enough. He has to correct for policy errors on the conservative side running across two decades – the six most wasteful years of the Howard government from 2001 to 2007, and the six combative years when Abbott led the Liberal Party from 2009 to 2015. The way government is run has to change along with the substance of policy. Turnbull conceded this point on the day of the challenge. "We need to restore traditional cabinet government," he said. "There must be an end to policy on the run and captain's calls. We need to be truly consultative with colleagues, members of parliament, senators and the wider public. We need an open government." For that to happen, Turnbull has to give up some of the self-defeating powers that his predecessors accumulated in the prime minister's office.

The tabloid critique of Abbott, and indeed Rudd, is that they were bonkers. It is made by MPs who claimed to be aware of their idiosyncrasies before casting a leadership ballot for them. Conveniently, they assumed these men would modify their behaviour after they won an election. The fulfilment of ambition, and the responsibility of government, was supposed to turn Abbott and Rudd into statesmen. Instead, success made them unaccountable. Both men challenged the very system they served by elevating their personal offices above the ministry and caucus. They behaved like presidents. It is uncanny how Turnbull's eloquent call to restore cabinet government echoed Gillard's plodding justification for taking Rudd's job five years earlier: a good government had lost its way.

Abbott and Rudd were not bad at politics. On the contrary, they were masters of campaigning, so skilled that they rewrote the rules. Abbott was elected prime minister despite his unpopularity. Rudd was the first Labor leader to win office when the economy was strong. Both men made perfect sense in Opposition, yet repeated their predecessor's mistakes. Rudd nailed Howard for wasting the proceeds of the mining boom, and then lost control of the budget after the global financial crisis. Abbott mocked the Rudd and Gillard soap opera, and then governed by yelling. Was either side actually paying attention in Opposition?

What these driven individuals could not grasp, refused even to countenance, was that an Australian prime minister does not have the formal power of a president. A president is directly elected by the people. This provides security of tenure. A president can only be removed by Congress in the most extraordinary circumstances. The US House of Representatives has impeached just two, at the rate of one per century: Andrew Johnson in 1868 and Bill Clinton in 1998. Both were acquitted by the Senate. Australian prime ministers are elected by the party room, and although they have more effective power than a president because they usually control the House of Representatives, they can be dismissed without warning when their colleagues fear losing office. A rapid turnover of leaders is not a recent affliction of our system. From the moment the Australian colonies were granted self-government in the 1850s, the most precarious position in the parliament was that of premier. In the first decade of federation, Australia swapped prime ministers seven times – from Barton to Deakin, then Watson, Reid, Deakin, Fisher, Deakin and Fisher. Only the first departure was voluntary. The next five changes occurred on the floor of the House of Representatives.

On a superficial level, the Rudd–Gillard–Abbott era matched the chaos. There were five prime ministers between 2010 and 2015, with only one change occurring at the ballot box, in 2013. But there was a crucial difference. In the federation's formative years, there was continuity in policy, from leader to leader, and from party to party. Deakin and Fisher were aligned on the biggest questions of the day: industry protection and the settling of wages through arbitration. (The sole exception was George Reid's Free Trade Party, which ruled for ten months between 1904 and 1905.)

With Rudd, Gillard and Abbott, entire programs were thrown out with the leader. And on the most vexing issue of all, climate change, each leader took several different positions. John Howard was no better. In government, he was an advocate for the original Kyoto protocol on climate change before he became an opponent, and was against emissions trading before he was for it.

I have no doubt that Rudd and Abbott sincerely believed their centralised approach was necessary, because their parties stood for little more than acquiring power. Ideas had to come from somewhere, and so it made sense to generate the big ones out of the prime minister's office. Rudd immersed himself in the paperwork. Abbott relied on his gut. But their decision-making was compromised by a shared insecurity. They wanted to be the smartest guy in the room, and so they cleared it of contrary viewpoints. Inevitably, policies became associated with the leader, not the party. The danger of throwing out policies along with the leader can be seen in how Gillard dealt with the mining tax. To prove that she was not Rudd, and that she could cut a deal with the mining companies, Gillard allowed them to design their own tax.

But there is danger in continuity for its own sake. Turnbull was wary of offending Abbott in an election year and so he limited the policy repudiation to the soft targets of his predecessor's obsessions. He terminated Abbott's imperial honours system, lifted the veto on wind farms, and declared the federal government once more willing to fund public transport infrastructure, science and innovation. This left Turnbull carrying the Abbott baggage on climate change and marriage equality. There would be no price on carbon pollution, or a parliamentary vote on same-sex marriage.

The difficulty for Turnbull, indeed for the entire system, is that too much is expected of the prime minister. The rhythm of politics today is the permanent volatility of the financial market. Messiah bubbles form around individuals, then burst. Then the speculators move on to the next saviour. Labor's Kevin07 campaign was the prototype for the leader as superhero. Rudd was the policy nerd who would restore serious government after the cynicism of Howard, and the Mandarin speaker who would keep the Chinese onside. A similar set of qualities were projected onto Turnbull. He was the suave intellect who would counter the small-mindedness of Abbott, and the merchant banker who would tame globalisation on our behalf. But this type of political celebrity can be a trap. The Rudd bubble ultimately burst because he would not lead. One non-decision was enough for people to write him off. When Rudd dumped his emissions trading scheme, voters concluded that he was just another politician.

On the previous two occasions when Australia reinvented itself, in the 1940s and 1980s, it was taken for granted that the project would be collaborative. Strong bonds of trust existed between politics, bureaucracy and the press, and between the representatives of labour, capital and welfare. Those connections have been broken by a culture that favours the attention-seeker over the expert, and the bully over the consensus-builder.

The debate we have to have is on the role of government in the economy. It is being forced on us by the market failures of the twenty-first century. Both sides cling defensively to the open model because it tells them a reassuring story of Australian success. But that open model has been exhausted by capitalism's extended crisis and the end of the mining boom. It cannot guarantee prosperity in the future without an active state. Once politicians understand this, they can release themselves from the spell cast by the leader they wish to be, Paul Keating.

The open model excels when the economy is strong, and in response to a global shock. But it struggles when the economy is in transition, because the market forces it is responding to are compromised. The four components of the model are a floating currency, low tariffs, interest rates set independently of the government, and wages determined directly by employers and workers above a minimum standard. Each is now delivering perverse results that are actually increasing the risk of recession.

For an uncomfortable period in 2012, and again in 2014, it seemed that the Australian dollar would not follow commodity prices down, leaving non-mining businesses gasping for air. The American car-makers used our overvalued currency as their excuse to quit the Australian market altogether. The goals of low tariffs were to flush out uncompetitive firms and release investment for globally minded businesses. It worked in the 1990s, but then mining crowded out all other activity. The boom ran from late 2003 to late 2011, with a brief pause during the global financial crisis. Now, on the other side of the mining cycle, investment is moving to the least productive part of the economy: housing. In normal times, the open model would respond with one, maybe two small rises in interest rates and a stern lecture from the governor of the Reserve Bank to prevent the market from overheating. But our central bank is hostage to a global experiment in very low interest rates designed to prop up the US and European economies. Those very low interest rates have seen property prices surge in Sydney. Any Australian politician who grasps the basics of our economic history should appreciate the danger of a housing bubble. Yet there has been a curious lack of engagement with this threat.

The final flaw in the open model is the enterprise bargaining system. It is excessively stingy at the moment because the balance of power has shifted too far towards the employer. In 2015 workers in the private sector received their smallest pay rise since the wages system was deregulated by Paul Keating. Surging house prices coupled with a squeeze on disposable incomes are the preconditions for a bust, but the open model can't resolve the conundrum.

A lever is missing, and it is one that governments forgot they still have control of: fiscal policy – the taxes they raise or lower, and the money they spend or invest. Fiscal policy briefly came back into fashion during the global financial crisis – in the form of the cash payments to consumers and the schools building program – only to fall out of favour again when Labor and the Coalition had a bipartisan panic attack over the budget deficit. Each side then pretended the crisis was over. Aggressive, then passive; these bewildering shifts in rhetoric from the treasurers became as unsettling as the sloganeering of the prime ministers.

All the elements of the open model operated with textbook efficiency in the global financial crisis. The currency tumbled, interest rates were slashed and employers spared their workers from mass retrenchment by reducing the hours they worked. The

Rudd government's cash handouts were effective because they complemented these measures. The need for fiscal policy now is to relieve the open model from a burden it was never designed for – managing an economy in transition. I am not arguing for stimulus to tide us over until capitalism resolves its crisis, but for a permanent change in the relationship between the state and the market. Government must reclaim responsibility for the areas of public policy that will prepare us for the future – most notably, education and infrastructure.

As a journalist I am wary of giving advice, especially when it involves a greater role for government in the economy. I can think of no generation of politicians I would trust less with the responsibility of redrawing the line between the market and the state than the current crop. But the choice is being forced on Australia anyway. The political system cannot restore public confidence without a more responsive government. And the economy won't stabilise without a more active government. The default setting of politics in the twenty-first century – to trust in the market – has proven to be bad economics, even for Australia, the only high-income nation to avoid the Great Recession. It has left us with gridlocked cities, growing inequality and a corporate sector that feels no obligation to pay tax. If politics waits any longer to address these issues, we will muddle into a recession and government will have to prop up the economy, but from a position of weakness, with the budget in deficit and interest rates too low to cut in a meaningful way.

This essay will explore how to augment the open model, based on the experience of the past fifteen years. The first step is to identify what is driving the big economic and cultural shifts of the era, both local and global. The changes are best understood by dividing the economy into its male and female sides.

Nation-Building

The Australian male has had a prosperous twenty-first century so far. Ignore the white-guy whinge about how women, and the Chinese, and the Indians, are pushing him to the sidelines of the culture. The unexpected story of the past decade and a half is the return of the full-time male worker. More than 1.6 million full-time jobs were created between 2000 and 2015, and for the first time since the 1960s the majority of those positions (more than 900,000) went to men.

The turnaround is not directly explained by the resources boom. The main engine of growth was construction, which was responsible for 300,000 of the 900,000 new full-time male jobs. Mining can claim an indirect stake in this activity through the many projects it generated, from the quarry to the port. But the greater influence was the residential property boom, which commenced in 1999, around four years before the rise of China. This should not come as a surprise.

It is the identity of the next largest employer which challenges the old assumption that the male side of the economy relies on brawn. More than 200,000 full-time male jobs were created in professional, scientific and technical services. These winners of the open economy include accountants, architects, computer programmers, lawyers, managers and scientific researchers. The number would have been even larger had the Australian Bureau of Statistics counted doctors and other medical specialists in this category, instead of in health care and social assistance.

Politics has no language to tell this story. It cuts against the foundation myth of Australia as the worker's paradise, where only men with blue collars need apply to define the nation's centre. White-collar workers comprised less than 4 per cent of male employees when the Hawke–Keating government first opened up the economy in the 1980s. Almost five times as many men worked in manufacturing back then. Manufacturing remained the dominant employer through the tectonic shifts of the 1980s and '90s, but it was losing ground to construction. It finally ceded top spot in 2006, and on present trends will drop to third, behind professional, scientific and technical services, either this year or in 2018. Ironically, the electoral implications are not appreciated by the professionals of the political class. The main parties still have their eyes fixed on the rear-view mirror of Howard's battlers, the term strategists used to describe the blue-collar males who switched from Labor to Liberal or Pauline Hanson in the 1990s. The Abbott government tried to revive them in the form of Tony's tradies, but this narrow macho pitch merely reminded the rest of the population that their prime minister did not relate to them.

The tertiary-educated men and women of Australia – let's call them Malcolm's graduates – are the underestimated voter of the twenty-first century. The main parties have tended to ignore them, despite their growing numbers, because they are assumed to be an alien species with no connection to ordinary Australians. In circular logic that only the political class could come up with, leaders have tried to play the elites off against the majority by talking down to the electorate. All this does is increase cynicism with politics, perpetuating the very problem the main parties were trying to fix – their declining primary vote. The poll numbers only improve when a party courts the blue-collar worker and the professional together, with an optimistic leader like Kevin Rudd or Malcolm Turnbull. The economics of our fractured modern workforce are even more challenging for the main parties. Although male jobs are diversifying, the concentration of blue-collar workers in construction creates a new set of risks that did not apply behind the tariff wall. Men who lost work in the protection era could expect to be rehired by the same employer, or at least in the same industry, in a recovery. That began to change in the recessions of the mid-1970s and early 1980s. By the early 1990s, the majority of the men who were laid off in that recession either left the workforce for good or became self-employed. The political system could barely contain their rage back then. How will it cope if their sons are laid off, when the main parties already face an existential threat from the Greens, independents and populists?

Construction is usually the first industry to shed staff in a downturn, and if the next recession is triggered by a housing bust, unemployment may climb too quickly for authorities to prevent a hard landing. Lay-offs in construction would set off a chain reaction of job losses in retail, which is already facing a severe challenge from online shopping. No one under the age of forty has any direct experience of the last crash in Australia, and we simply don't know how this generation would respond to a soft or hard landing, given the debts it is carrying. Household debt was 70 per cent of household income in 1990. Today it is more than double that – 187 per cent.

The danger to social cohesion multiplies because the resources boom has already hollowed out other industries. The 140,000 new jobs created in mining since 2000 matched an almost identical loss of jobs in manufacturing. As mining inevitably contracts, where will these men go next? They cannot simply return to their old workplace, because many of those businesses have closed down.

The manufacturing job losses of the past five years are comparable to those caused by the early 1990s recession. Another round of mass retrenchments is likely as Holden and Toyota wind up their Australian operations in 2017. The question the Turnbull government should be asking itself before the property market cools, before Clive Palmer shuts down another venture, and before the car industry disappears, is whether the public sector can find work for tens of thousands of blue-collar men before they become a political wrecking ball.

The answer is to put them to work on major infrastructure projects, restoring government to the part of the economy it should never have abandoned in the name of deregulation. This is one of the magic keys of policy that can unlock Australian potential: public investment in areas such as transport, communications and water security. It might even release politics from its obsessions with media management and factional intrigue. Once the state resumes responsibility for the things the market either can't deliver, or delivers at unreasonable cost to taxpayers, the focus of politics shifts from game-playing back to nation-building. Inevitably, some bad decisions will be made with public funds, but the time has long passed when that was a plausible reason not to act.

The running down of infrastructure has been a sore point with voters for at least a decade. They understood the economics better than the politicians. As their lives sped up, their communities succumbed to gridlock, slowing the trip from home to work, to school and to the child-care centre. But the system has struggled to correct itself because the capacity of government to invest in the economy has been diminished by years of neglect. Another monster was created during the government's absence from the real economy. When the main parties embraced the market in the 1980s and '90s by selling public assets and winding back investment in infrastructure, they left an opening where the state once was. The theory was that funds would be freed for more productive investments in the private sector. It was only half-right. Public investment fell from around 8 per cent of gross domestic product in the mid-1980s to around 4 per cent from the late '90s on. Half that opening was filled by business investment, but the other half went to bricks and mortar. This transaction came to define the Howard era, and by the middle of 2000 the property sector was substantially larger than the public sector, contributing a record 6.7 per cent of GDP compared to 4.6 per cent for public investment. In effect, we were building new housing estates and apartment blocks without train lines or schools to service them.

That particular spike in activity was unsustainable, because the industry was trying to beat the introduction of the GST on 1 July 2000. Construction froze in the second half of 2000, and the economy almost went into recession because of it. The message an economist would have drawn from this episode was beware the property cycle. Not John Howard. He doubled the first home owner's grant, and the patient had their fever restored. By 2003, property investment was worth 6.2 per cent of GDP compared to 4.1 per cent for public investment. Housing maintained its lead through the first phase of the mining boom, a distortion Howard further encouraged by returning revenue windfalls to taxpayers, instead of using some of that money for infrastructure.

The global financial crisis was supposed to provide the reset that would bring government back into the field. In the earliest days of the crisis, the Rudd government made an offer to the states it thought would be too good to refuse. Give us your pending list of infrastructure projects and the federal government will help fund them. An embarrassed silence followed. Treasury secretary Ken Henry explains: "Not one government in Australia had even one infrastructure project sitting in its top drawer, ready for investment – not even one." Staggering, because the common complaint of every Labor state regime against the former Howard government was that infrastructure had been short-changed.

Rudd would not be deterred. His second stimulus package, announced in February 2009, contained more cash payments and the most ambitious government infrastructure program since the Snowy Mountains Scheme: the schools building program. It was designed to support construction employment until the crisis had passed, and proved to be quite successful. But at the time it suffered from guilt by association with the pink batts insulation scheme.

I still marvel at Tony Abbott's oppositionist brilliance in 2010. He shifted the blame for a global recession onto the government that had managed to avoid it. All it required was a simple reframing of the argument from jobs saved to money wasted, and for Labor to lose itself in the personality clash between Kevin Rudd and Julia Gillard.

What the schools building program actually achieved, and where it fell short of its promise, should be of interest to policy-makers around the world. It is a perfect case study of government intervention through infrastructure, because the money flowed relatively quickly.

Construction jobs fell by 18,000 in the year after the global financial crisis. Although a relatively small decline by the standards of past recessions, it was nonetheless the first such fall in eight years.

The schools building program could do nothing about those lay-offs. The test is what happened to employment in the following year, and the news was very good. More than 50,000 people were hired. The contribution of the schools building program could also be seen in the national accounts. Public investment had been 5.2 per cent of GDP when the scheme was announced. It increased in each of the next four quarters and peaked at 6.7 per cent in the March quarter of 2010. Private investment collapsed over the same period, from 16.1 per cent of GDP to 14.3 per cent, while housing investment remained more or less steady.

Case closed. Except that Labor could not make that case to the electorate. This meant the Coalition could continue to proclaim the opposite: that Labor had been reckless with public funds. Unfortunately, the Coalition believed its own spin and did not see the need to increase spending.

Tony Abbott took office with private investment at 16.9 per cent of GDP, and public and housing investment each at 4.7 per cent. If he had understood the risk, he would have fast-tracked some infrastructure projects. Instead, he did nothing. Two years later, as Abbott joined Gillard and Rudd in the political past tense, private investment had dropped to 14.1 per cent of GDP and public investment to 4.1 per cent. All that was holding up the investment side of the economy was bricks and mortar, which was being supported by low interest rates. Housing investment reached 5.6 per cent of GDP – its highest level since before the global financial crisis. No matter how many times politicians say they want to invest in the future, they lack the discipline to follow through. Abbott wanted to be known as Australia's infrastructure prime minister, but evinced little interest in the topic while in office.

The tragedy here is that our leaders refuse to learn from experience. The schools building program was policy on the run. It helped the economy in the short term, but was it the most productive investment the government could have made at the time? We don't know because, as Ken Henry says, there wasn't a decent list of projects to choose from.

The IMF chided the Abbott government in 2015 for tightening public spending when the economy needed support. In response to this criticism, according to the IMF, "[the government] concurred that addressing infrastructure bottlenecks was a key priority and funding of high quality infrastructure projects was a key focus. They also pointed to substantial existing planned investments, including the national broadband network, with total general government investment over coming years expected to remain above levels of the 1990s and early 2000s." Kevin Rudd might have afforded himself a chuckle that the NBN was put forward as an example of Coalition intervention.

The scale of the problem is only partly acknowledged in the government's response. Maintaining public investment "above the levels of the 1990s and early 2000s" will not give the nation the infrastructure it needs. If Australia is to catch up, spending should probably return to the levels of the 1960s, when it was closer to 10 per cent of GDP. It is no use pretending that the private sector can deliver physical infrastructure such as rail lines or roads better than the government. The market has had two decades to prove otherwise, and its legacy is congestion. This is not to suggest there is no role for the private sector, or that in areas such as technology or energy the government should revive the old, discredited policy of picking winners. The lines do not need to be redrawn. The existing model – where government provides support for innovation through subsidies, but leaves it to the scientists and other experts to come up with the ideas, and the private sector to bring them to consumers – works well. But government must take the lead on physical infrastructure. Only it has an economy-wide perspective. The market, left to its own devices, will only build houses.

John Howard was fond of asserting that there was no infrastructure crisis in Australia, and even if there was, it was the fault of the Labor states. There was a good deal of truth to the second part of this observation. Responsibility for infrastructure is shared among federal, state and even local governments. The federal government has sole jurisdiction over telecommunications, while electricity, dams, water supply, sewerage, ports and public transport are in the hands of the states. Road and rail are the key areas of overlap, and it is here that the trivial rivalries of federation have caused the greatest economic damage.

The state that claims to have the most innovative policy record in the new millennium also provides the best illustration of what went wrong on infrastructure. Victorians can't say they didn't see the issue coming. The Coalition government of Jeff Kennett and the Labor government of Steve Bracks were a decade ahead of the nation in promoting a high-migration future for their state when every other mainland government was dabbling in Hansonism. Even Bob Carr, the unashamedly cosmopolitan New South Wales premier, played the low-migration card, declaring Sydney full at the turn of the twenty-first century.

Victoria wanted people, yet when they came the Bracks government didn't build fast enough to cater for them. Labor couldn't connect the dots between the realisation of its dream for a big Victoria and the public transport network that would be needed to service it. Money and time were wasted on an infuriating electronic ticketing system, when what the state really needed was to expand Melbourne's train network.

Joel Deane chronicled the mistakes in his book on the Victorian Labor government, *Catch and Kill.* He quotes transport minister Peter Batchelor, who suggests the government had trouble focusing on the biggest issue before it:

> Each year there tended to be an area of government that would do exceptionally well out of the budget. It would be schools one year, or

> hospitals the next, and the metropolitan public transport was left too late and the difficulty with public metropolitan train services [is] they take so long to bring to fruition. So, if you don't start early you never get anywhere near it to compete [with the increased patronage].

Steve Bracks told Deane that the problem began with the state's treasury department consistently underestimating both population growth and the effect this growth would have on passenger numbers.

> Our policy was to lift the use of public transport from 30, 40 per cent, whatever it was, to 80 per cent ... Those targets became totally irrelevant as our population continued to boom and our employment levels continued to grow, which meant people were commuting to jobs in the city.

It was only late in the life of the government that public transport received attention in the budget. But John Brumby, treasurer under Bracks and by now premier, still did not see it as an election-decider. That misreading of community sentiment ensured Labor would lose every seat along the Frankston train line in the 2010 campaign, and with them, office. The new Coalition government did not believe public transport mattered all that much either. Its priority was roads, and in the 2014 election, voters dispatched a second government in a row, returning Labor to power after a single term in Opposition.

By now, the political argument for public investment should roll off the tongue. Infrastructure promotes growth, and maintains social cohesion by keeping people connected. When the economy is weak, it has the bonus of saving jobs.

With experience, governments can use their projects to augment the open model. Spending could be boosted when the private sector is weak. The NBN would be an ideal vehicle for a flexible fiscal policy. However, the Coalition has been slow to take up this opportunity because its tribal instinct is to squeeze the programs of its Labor predecessor in order to free up funds for its own agenda. To date, no level of government has cleared the practical obstacles of project selection and implementation. The electoral cycle runs too quickly for the investment cycle, and until the parties adopt a more mature approach, each new government will be condemned to repeat the errors of its predecessor as it tries to rewrite the nation's infrastructure policy from scratch.

***

The volatility on the male side of the economy can be moderated once government rediscovers the lost art of planning. The policy challenges on the female side are more complex. Job security is not the issue, because as the population ages there will be more work in health care and social assistance. This sector was responsible for one in three of the 1.5 million jobs created for women over the past fifteen years, and is now the single largest employer in the nation.

Note how the economy is distributing labour in every direction. Behind the tariff wall of old Australia, three of the top five employers were working-class and predominantly male – manufacturing, construction and agriculture. Now three of the top five are pink-collar, including the two largest employers. Women hold the majority of jobs in health care and social assistance (80 per cent), retail (55 per cent) and education (70 per cent). Only one of the top five is blue-collar – construction, which is 90 per cent male.

The relative improvement in male full-time work over the past fifteen years has not slowed the feminisation of the workforce. The biggest shift has been from full-time male work to part-time female work. More than 80 per cent of all jobs were full-time when the dollar was floated in December 1983. In the intervening thirty-two years, that proportion has shrunk from 82.6 per cent to 69.1 per cent. Although men still hold the majority of those full-time jobs, they are now outnumbered by all women in work, either full-time or part-time.

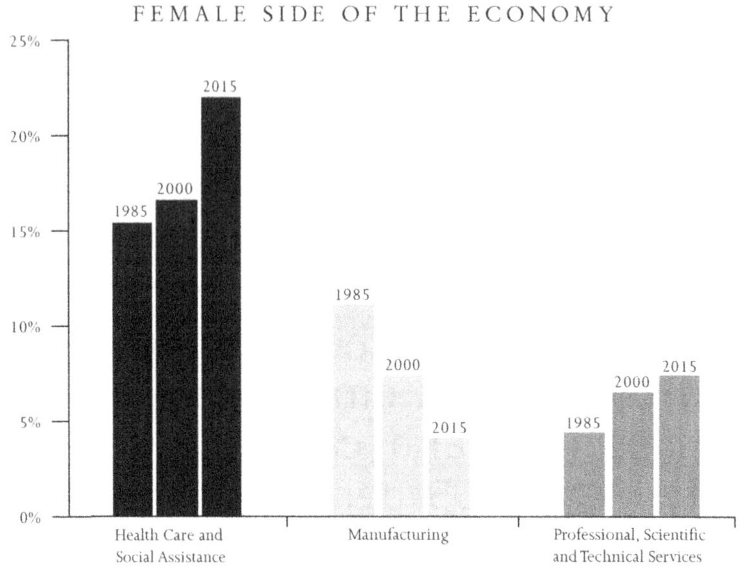

What is wrong with this picture is that deregulation has yet to unleash the full potential of the better-educated half of Australian society. Women are marginalised in work, even as they become numerically dominant. Across all sectors, they are still paid less for doing the same work as men, and the jobs the economy is generating for them tend to be at the lower end of the income scale.

There is another aspect to consider. We are one of just three developed nations where part-time work accounts for more than 30 per cent of all jobs. Only the Netherlands and Switzerland have higher rates of casualisation than Australia. In Canada, the economy most like ours, part-time work is just under 20 per cent; in New Zealand it is below 25 per cent. Our settler cousins also boast notably higher rates of female employment than ours.

An optimist would read these differences as an opportunity. If Australia could move its female employment rate up to match Canada's, and reduce its casualisation rate towards New Zealand's, the boost to the economy would be substantial. But what if these differences reflect a national hang-up about gender? Australia's political culture remains doggedly macho. Tony Abbott could only find room for one woman in his first nineteen-member cabinet; Canada's conservative leader Stephen Harper had six out of twenty-six when he took office in 2006. Malcolm Turnbull's first cabinet had five women out of twenty-one, again well short of the new Canadian standard of fifteen out of thirty-one under Prime Minister Justin Trudeau. Asked why he wanted gender equality, Trudeau replied: "Because it is 2015." By their own example, the governments of Abbott and Turnbull devalue female participation in work. To close the gap with our peers, politics may first need to undergo its own feminisation, so the ministry and the wider parliament more closely resemble the society they serve.

Australia's high rates of part-time work reveal a further uncomfortable truth about the open economy: the pendulum swing of power from labour to capital. Employer associations have been beating their chests for decades about the supposed high cost of labour in Australia. The argument was valid in the Whitlam–Fraser era, when wages surged to historic highs and profits were reduced to their lowest level as a proportion of national income on record. Wages accounted for more than 60 per cent of national income between 1974 and 1978 and again in 1982–83. Both episodes were associated with industrial mayhem and deep recessions, and they have distorted the conservative view of the world ever since. I lost count of the number of stories my old newspaper, the *Australian,* and its rival the *Australian Financial Review* ran under the headline "Wages break-out." There was never any data to support the scare.

The open model was designed to restore the profits of employers, and on any impartial reading of the evidence it has overshot. In the full employment 1960s, business profits averaged 20 per cent of national income. In each decade of deregulation, the profit share has been above that, averaging 24 per cent at the end of the 1980s, 25 per cent in the 1990s, 26 per cent on the eve of the global financial crisis and spiking to 28 per cent with the second mining boom. Each percentage point gain for capital has been at the expense of labour.

Yet the urge to blame the worker has not passed. Weekend penalty rates are a favourite target. Hotels and restaurants claim more of them would open for business on Sundays if they could pay their staff the weekday rate. Perhaps, but it does not follow that the economy would be better off, let alone the young waiter whose take-home pay is likely to be cut. Household consumption is the beating heart of any economy. It accounts for more than half of Australia's

GDP, and should not be restricted without good reason. Accommodation and food services employ more than 800,000 workers. Many would be worse off without penalty rates. Their loss of spending power would need to be at least matched by greater consumption by the rest of the population to leave the economy no worse off. I can't see it happening in the present environment. What has been holding back households since the global financial crisis is not the lack of opportunities to spend, but the debts they are carrying. A seventh day of consumption might help cafés, but the money that flows there will be offset by cutbacks on other discretionary items.

This is a small example of a one-sided conversation between the business lobby and the public. There is virtually no support in the community for the abolition of weekend penalty rates. Not even Tony Abbott would fly this flag for business. But the open model has indulged capital to the point where it confuses its own pecuniary interest with the national good. One of the most glaring manifestations of this is the salaries that company executives pay themselves. This is where the real wages break-out is occurring. Another area of justified alarm is corporate tax avoidance. Business has convinced itself that globalisation means it owes no obligation to society other than to generate profit. When capital took this attitude in the past, either the economic cycle took care of the greed with a recession, or the political system pulled rank. Usually it was both, with the economic crisis prompting the political correction. The global financial crisis has not followed this script, at least to date. If anything, business has become more presumptuous since 2008. Give us a cut in the company tax rate. Fund it with an increase in the GST. There is no economic logic here, only ambit claim.

We are reliving one of the most toxic aspects of the 1970s, when trade unions responded to the global shock of rising inflation by asking for more money, thus killing the jobs of their members. Today it is business which holds the upper hand in the workplace, and it is abusing that privilege at the expense of the wider economy. Every demand for concessions becomes a test of the system, just as with the strikes of the 1970s. This is greed driven by an inferiority complex. Australian firms cannot have much faith in the future if their response to competition from Asia is to ask government for even more power over workers.

Both sides of politics have fallen for the line that in order to maintain our record run of prosperity you have to squeeze the employee, the student, the single parent, the consumer – anyone, really, who does not run a business or own an investment property. It is not unreasonable for politicians to want us to be match-fit for globalisation. But whenever they deliver this message, they do so as an admonition, not a call to arms, and without proposing any clear trade-offs.

Australians are reasonably comfortable with the open economy, provided the government knows whose side it is on. But they don't like change forced on them without explanation, or the buttering-up that follows once government realises it has little support for a policy. Howard rushed WorkChoices through the Senate when he had the balance of power, hoping voters would forget about it by the time of the next election. They didn't. He eventually apologised, and watered down his legislation so they would be no worse off, but they didn't forgive him.

In a sense, the anxiety about the future begins as a panic of elites. The institutions of politics, media and business remain older, whiter and more masculine than the nation itself. Their response to increased diversity is counterintuitive. The parties know they have to lift their primary vote, news organisations know they have to replenish their ageing audiences, businesses know they have to find new customers. Yet they react to a loss of market share by throwing a tantrum on behalf of what remains of their base, thus reinforcing the loss of market share. When Labor and Liberal politicians ask me why the *Australian* has become so strident in recent years, I remind them that it is behaving no differently to their parties.

Politics is trapped in an old economy mindset while simultaneously advocating for an open economy. Labor wishes collars were still blue, and the Coalition would be happier if Australia could preserve its traditional Anglo identity. Yet income inequality, a diverse but less secure workforce and a rapidly changing ethnic mix are unavoidable features of globalisation. In response, our politicians routinely pick the wrong fights. The contradiction can only be reconciled if we assume the worst: that neither side understands economics as well as it thinks it does. They defer to the market when they should intervene, and they push against our new Eurasian identity when they should embrace it.

Ken Henry says the political system has failed to respond to the challenge of a growing population:

> It's unclear to me to what extent people engaging in policy thinking, including in infrastructure thinking, understand what it is that Australia is facing. What Australia's future really is. I don't want to alarm people with the population projections, but they're out there anyway ... In the second half of the twentieth century, in those five decades, the Australian population increased by between 2.1 million and 2.4 million people [per decade]. In the first decade of this century the Australian population increased by 3 million people. According to the mid-case projections, in each of the next four decades, the Australian population is going to grow by between 3.8 and 4.1 million. That's in each of those decades. Now, I was secretary to the Treasury during pretty much the first decade of this century, and one of the things that was very evident to me was that coping with an increase in the Australian population of 3

> million people was more than the Australian policy system could handle.

He says congestion on the roads of Sydney and Melbourne has already reached "unacceptable levels" and is affecting the quality of life in both cities, even as incomes have grown.

> The pressure on urban amenity generally in Sydney in particular, but also to some extent in Melbourne; the pressure being placed on house prices and housing affordability in Sydney and Melbourne and indeed in other cities around the country; the pressure on environmental amenity of new housing sub-divisions being opened up in places where no sane person would ever locate a house, but we're doing it – those sorts of pressures we found ourselves dealing with in the first decade of the twenty-first century, and that was dealing with an increase of 3 million people. There is insufficient comprehension of the magnitude of the task that we confront.

Politicians understand that they need to take infrastructure seriously; their focus groups tell them so. But the very conduct of politics guarantees poor investment decisions, regardless who funds the projects. It is common now for an incoming federal or state government to have a competing wish-list that was drawn up in a political office – and not, as Henry wanted, after a proper market evaluation.

With politics setting the priorities, a change of government inevitably means that existing projects are either cancelled, or slowed to make room in the budget for a new agenda. Once again, it is Victoria which set the benchmark for dysfunction.

Before public transport, the pressing infrastructure need in the state was water security. The Coalition first argued for a desalination plant at the 2006 election, as a response to what had become the worst drought in the state's history. But the Bracks government was not persuaded. It changed its mind after the election, and in 2007 embraced the idea. But then the Coalition turned from champion to opponent. The plant was completed in late 2012 under the new government, but was effectively mothballed early in the new year, with the Coalition water minister reportedly making it his "personal goal" never to order any water from the plant. Imagine Robert Menzies completing Ben Chifley's Snowy Mountain Scheme, then refusing to take any irrigation water or electricity from it. The Victorian pettiness extended to the Metro Rail Project, which was originally identified as a priority in 2008 by an independent report chaired by businessman Rod Eddington. The Coalition government re-evaluated this project along with all others, and in 2014 came up with its own plan, which lapsed with its election defeat that year. In 2015 the new Labor government returned to the original proposal. In those seven years of draft and redraft very little actual work was done.

The federal government has its own interest in interference, because it holds the credit card. And when a government is as overtly political as Tony Abbott's was, the decision to invest is brazenly tribal. Abbott wanted to lock in the Victorian Coalition plan for the East–West Link, and allocated funding before all the contracts had been signed. It suited him to spend the money early, because it made the last federal Labor budget deficit appear larger than it would otherwise have been.

Both sides saw the 2014 state election as a referendum on the project, and when voters threw out the Coalition, the new Labor government assumed that it had won the argument. But Abbott insisted he would only support the Coalition's program, effectively leaving Victoria without any federal funding for public transport in 2015. Meanwhile, Labor had to pay almost a billion dollars in compensation to the consortium that would have built the project under the Coalition. So Victorian taxpayers were short-changed twice, once by the Coalition and once by Labor, all in the name of politics.

At this point in the cycle, when the economy is slowing and federal and state budgets are in deficit, politicians are more risk-averse. They are likely to see congestion back-to-front, as the fault of excessive population growth rather than poor government planning. The populist and the environmentalist can find common cause here: one protests against the influx of migrants, the other fights the apartment towers.

Luckily we have the Bob Carr example to debunk the urban myth that low growth is somehow more sustainable. Let's take the ten years after the *Tampa* and the declaration that Sydney was full, and see what happened. New South Wales Labor mastered politics, and little else. The party machine suffocated the state with its corruption. The dog days for New South Wales were salad days for the rest of the nation. The Australian economy grew by 3.1 per cent on average between 2002 and 2011, from the eve of the mining boom to its end. Every state and territory shared the spoils, except one. New South Wales trailed at just under 2 per cent, far enough behind the rest that the responsibility must rest largely with its government. Nor did low growth make New South Wales more cohesive. While the rest of the nation partied, Sydney exploded with violence across the income spectrum: the white middle class rioted at Cronulla, the white underclass at Macquarie Fields and the black underclass at Redfern.

Demography had the last laugh on Labor. The state that trialled the low-growth option became *more* diverse, as local-born refugees from the Sydney property market moved to Queensland, Western Australia, Victoria and even Tasmania, while a new wave of educated migrants from China and India replaced them. Total population growth slowed, but

Sydney became the most cosmopolitan city in the nation.

Today, 39 per cent of Sydney's population are overseas-born, and another 25 per cent have at least one parent who is a migrant. In Perth, the first generation are 37 per cent of the population and the second generation another 25 per cent. In Melbourne, the respective figures are 35 per cent and 24 per cent. The last time migrants accounted for more than a third of the total population of any major settlement was in the 1870s.

The reason there is no complacent middle for Australia to aim at is that our continued prosperity is dependent on mass migration. The experiences of Melbourne and Sydney are two sides of the same essential risk. If governments do not plan ahead of that growth, eventually it will overwhelm them.

Australia presently has four world-class cities ranked in the top ten for "liveability" – Melbourne first, Adelaide equal fifth, Sydney seventh and Perth ninth. "Those that score best tend to be mid-sized cities in wealthier countries with a relatively low population density," the *Economist* Intelligence Unit explains. "These can foster a range of recreational activities without leading to high crime levels or overburdened infrastructure."

The evidence from overseas suggests that cities start to become unliveable – that is, gridlocked, polluted and with higher rates of crime and widening gaps between rich and poor – once their population exceeds four or five million. Sydney and Melbourne are approaching that threshold. Australia can only defy the trend if it takes nation-building seriously.

Although Australian governments need to return to pre-deregulation levels of investment in infrastructure, this area of public policy has become too important to leave to politicians. A Reserve Bank– style model is required to identify and rank projects on economic and social grounds, and to recommend timelines for implementation. Politics can then decide which infrastructure to support, and put the case to the public based on independent analysis. Ideally, this system should aim for continuity of investment between governments. If contracts are to be broken, voters should know the cost ahead of an election. The states will need their treasurers to think more like planning ministers; federal treasurers will have to re-educate themselves, and the public, about the value of government borrowing.

Inevitably there will be competition between public and private sectors for investment funds, and for construction workers. The onus is on governments to have projects configured in a way that causes least harm. This should go without saying, but, as we've seen, the conduct of politics often delivers the most perverse results. The key is to think ahead, and for governments to be prepared to dial spending up when the economy is slow, and dial it back down when it is strong. That way, public investment helps to smooth the economic cycle. There is, however, a catch: the federal budget is currently almost as broken as the nation's infrastructure.

The Howard Gift

Australia did not need to have a decade of budget deficits. We were one of the few rich nations that could profit from the global savings imbalance between China and the United States. Unlike the Americans, we had something the Chinese wanted. One simple contrast shows our advantage. In the ten years from 2005 to 2014, Australia exported $150 billion more to China than it imported – essentially coal and iron going out and computers and large-screen TVs coming in. The Americans accumulated a trade deficit to the Chinese of $2,735 billion over the same period.

Paul Volcker, the celebrated chair of the US Federal Reserve who broke the back of US stagflation in the 1980s, likens the global financial crisis to the earlier Latin American debt crisis. The genesis was the same. A new player entered the global economy with a big bank balance. In the 1970s it was the oil-rich Arab states. "People [were] watching all that money [and asking] how do we recycle it?" he tells me. "Well, they recycled it to Latin America via the big banks. And so there was this big flow of liquidity, which was pleasant when it happened."

The financial institutions thought they were doing Latin American countries a favour by funding their economic development with cheap credit. But it wasn't sustainable. Volcker had a hand in the reckoning. His cure for stagflation was very high interest rates, which hurt the Latin Americans, among others. "But they were going to have a crisis anyway," Volcker says. "It was just a question of time, because they ran out of lenders. Eventually some lender says, 'No, I don't want to lend anymore,' which is what happened in Mexico. So one big lender said that and the others stopped and suddenly you had a crisis where six months earlier everybody was lending like crazy."

> Well, go ahead to the 2000s and you have this big disequilibrium from the United States deficit, from the growing Chinese and Japanese surpluses. But the money flowed and the [deficits] all got financed very easily. What's the worry?
>
> The hardest thing in the world is to take restraining action when things are going very well. You've got no political support for it. They say: 'What are you doing? You're crazy, you know things are going smoothly, let it rip. Don't do anything to disturb the stock market or drive up interest rates or close the budget deficit, we're ok.' It's all very pleasant until something in the chain of financial transactions, which become more and more complex, snaps, and in our case of course it was a subprime mortgage and the mortgage market.

The global financial crisis was a replay of the 1970s, but with three substantial plot twists. First, the money flowed from an emerging economy to the richest nation on earth, which then recycled the money through increasingly dodgy loans. Second, within Europe, the funds travelled from its richest member, Germany, to nations with long histories of victimhood, Greece and Ireland. The third act, which is yet to be written, will be the reckoning for China as it deflates its own credit bubble and shifts its economy away from exports to domestic consumption.

***

A national budget does not necessarily reflect the real economy, but it is a gauge of public values and political temperament. Australia approached the twenty-first century with uncharacteristic prudence. While the Bush administration pushed the US federal budget into deficit to fund massive personal tax cuts, the Howard government took the old-fashioned approach. Income-tax cuts were paid for with a new tax on consumption – the goods and services tax – and Australia's budget remained in surplus. The total tax take was actually a little higher in 2002–03 than it had been in the last year of the old tax system, 1999–2000. It was the ideal fiscal platform from which to greet the rise of China.

In his enthusiasm to sell the GST, John Howard declared that taxpayers would be spared from future bracket creep, the process by which inflation pushes taxpayers up the scales. The worker on average earnings would face a marginal tax rate no higher than 30 cents in the dollar, and no more than 20 per cent of taxpayers would face the top two rates of 42 and 47 cents in the dollar. "You can almost call it the 'bracket creep abolition provision' of the tax plan," he declared, after securing the senate's support for the GST. It was an impossible standard to meet, and as the 2004 election approached, Howard was anxious to adjust the tax scales so that Labor could not accuse him of breaking his promise. That year, I had commissioned research for the *Australian* to show how much tax the government owed workers in bracket creep. By 2005–06, it would be $3.8 billion, if the government did not act. In the 2004 budget Peter Costello obliged with a tax cut worth $3.8 billion by 2005–06. He made a point of underlining the figure when he talked to a huddle of *Australian* reporters at the media lock-up for the budget. The policy nerd in me was chuffed to have got the number right.

If this process had been repeated every few years, no lasting harm would have been done to the budget. But just as these tax cuts landed, the budget also began to catch the first of the revenue windfalls from China. The nation's finances suddenly assumed the character of a magic pudding, as tax collections from companies and investors soared to unprecedented levels. Each time the forecasts were updated, the surplus was larger than expected, even after the tax cuts. At subsequent lock-ups Costello would tell us that some households couldn't have their taxes cut any further, so new payments had to be invented for them, so they wouldn't miss out on the next round. At each budget from 2005 to 2007, the tax cuts went well beyond bracket creep, and they were not offset by savings from elsewhere. The government assumed the China-led surge in revenue was permanent, and the additional income raised from companies and investors could be returned to workers without risking the bottom line. The total tax take didn't change in this period, but the personal tax burden was now at its lowest level since the 1970s, and it still had further to fall, because Howard had one final tax cut to announce at the 2007 election.

It was too good to be true, of course. Once the global financial crisis struck, the taxes paid by companies and investors collapsed. Of itself, this was not unusual. As boom turns to bust, businesses and their shareholders are more likely to report losses, not profits, on their tax returns. But the personal tax cuts relied on elevated levels of company tax and capital gains tax. Once those props were removed, the budget imploded.

In the Whitlam and Fraser recessions, budget revenue maintained its share of GDP because of bracket creep. In Keating's recession, revenue did drop sharply, but then it recovered with the economy. Again, bracket creep was the key.

This time, revenue fell further, despite low unemployment, and did not bounce back, despite there being no recession. Treasurers on both sides of politics struggled to explain why. Here is Wayne Swan, in his 2013 budget speech: "While our economy remains resilient, powerful global forces and the stubbornly high Australian dollar have savaged budget revenues."

And Joe Hockey in 2015: "In the past twelve months we have coped well with weaker than expected global demand, lower commodity prices and falling revenue. Even in the face of the largest fall in our terms of trade in half a century, which has contributed to a significant fall in tax receipts, our economic plan has helped Australia to have one of the fastest growing economies in the developed world."

These were distractions. The truth is that the problem was home-grown. The decade-long run of personal tax cuts removed the budget's automatic repair mechanism: bracket creep. This is why revenue contracted so sharply, even though the economy was still growing.

THE HOWARD GIFT

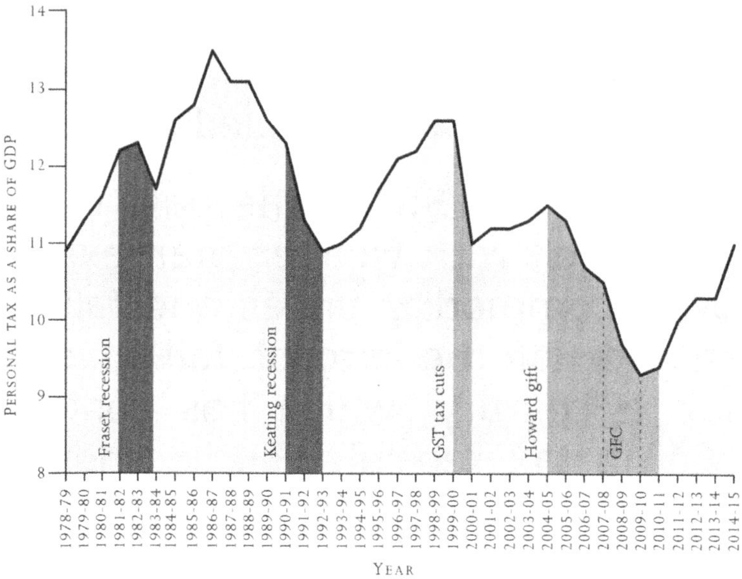

In an ideal world, workers who had kept their jobs through a down-turn and those who had taken jobs in a recovery would pay more as inflation pushed them up the income-tax scales, until the point where surplus is restored. Only then should tax cuts be considered. Instead Howard and Rudd gave all taxpayers much more than bracket creep would have taken. The National Centre for Social and Economic Modelling put the excess tax cuts at between $20 billion and $31.5 billion per year (depending on the criteria used).

Labor would have balanced the budget in 2012–13 if it had the foresight to cancel just those tax cuts promised in the 2007 election campaign. The political opportunity to do so presented itself during the global financial crisis. The government could have sold the two stimulus payments as a more responsible version of the tax cuts – a larger upfront benefit which did not damage the structure of the budget. But the option was never seriously considered, because Rudd was determined to keep all his promises, to the letter. Even if it had been, the fiscal reward would have been temporary. The hole in the budget was deeper than just one round of unfunded tax cuts and the deficit would have returned in the following year.

Australia does not have a budget crisis, not in the American or European sense of the term. Our taxes and spending remain at the modest end of the spectrum compared to other rich nations. But we have failed to live up to our own previous high standard of prudence.

Ken Henry says that it was not apparent during the mining boom that the tax cuts would be unsustainable, because the budget surplus would always end up higher than forecast. "If you knew for a fact that the revenue surge was going to be temporary, then the smartest thing to do, in fact the only sensible thing to do really, would be to bank the lot of it, put it in the sovereign wealth fund. No question about it." But Henry and his colleagues thought at least some of the extra revenue was permanent, and so it could be safely given back to workers. With hindsight, he says there were two parts of the revenue surge that were not permanent: capital gains, which is counted under personal income tax; and company tax.

> So should we have known that? It is certainly arguable that we should have known it. But every time the government put out a budget or a budget update from 2003–04 through to 2007–08, the government had to admit to the Australian population that revenue was much, much more buoyant than what they'd been saying it was. Even though they were providing big income tax cuts and increases in family payments along the way. Very difficult in that environment to firstly convince yourself that it's only temporary and then, if you have convinced yourself, you've got to turn around and convince everybody else in the room that what appears to be happening is not actually happening.

John Howard and Peter Costello did not consciously set out to make the income-tax system an agent for inequality. They thought the reverse would occur: by reducing the burden on the top, everyone would want to climb the ladder. No one doubted the theory in the government or the bureaucracy. Tax cuts were supposed to reward effort, and to encourage people to save and invest.

Costello lifted the threshold to the point where only 2 per cent of tax-payers paid the top rate by 2007–08. This is what made the tax system less progressive. Many higher income earners suddenly found they were paying the marginal tax rate of 30 cents that was meant for average earners.

If the tax cuts had encouraged Australia to work harder, economists could say they were worth the trouble. But productivity stalled during this period, which begs the question whether all that money made us soft. One thing is clear, though: the tax cuts made Australia less fair.

We know this now because of a fascinating study undertaken by Nicolas Herault and Francisco Azpitarte for the Brotherhood of St Laurence and the Melbourne Institute of Applied Economic and Social Research. They looked at the period of our greatest prosperity, from the late 1990s to the eve of the global financial crisis, and found that, measured in take-home pay, inequality increased. The Howard government tax cuts were not the only reason, but they were a significant factor. "We find that the direct effect of tax-transfer policy reforms accounts for approximately half of the observed increase in income inequality over this period," they wrote.

This is the part of the Great Recession we did not avoid. We had imported the American disease of budget-busting tax cuts for the rich. The point here is that rising inequality is not always the result of market failure: it may also be due to government failure. It is true that politicians no longer have an influence on wages beyond the minimum rate. The open model effectively sets the market rate. But politicians still influence disposable income through the tax and payments system. That will never change, and nor should it in a democracy.

What is striking in retrospect is that Treasury, and the governments of Howard, Rudd, Gillard and Abbott, convinced themselves that the budget was basically out of their hands. Not even the global financial crisis changed that thinking. The emergency was deemed to be temporary. The government should only provide stimulus for a year or two – after that, the budget was supposed to go back into neutral gear, neither slowing nor speeding up the economy.

By degrees, the Coalition and Labor convinced themselves that they were absolved of responsibility for the mood swings of a China-dominated global economy. The revenue windfall could be given away, and when it disappeared the deficit could be blamed on the rest of the world.

The Howard Gift was not easily retrieved, because the economy remained sluggish after the global financial crisis. Any repair to the revenue side of the budget had to be offset with compensation to ensure that households continued to spend and businesses continued to hire. The Gillard government followed this risk-averse script by giving back more than it collected from the carbon and mining taxes.

With the personal tax scales considered off-limits, Labor looked to the spending side of the budget and, in doing so, reinforced the unfairness of the Howard Gift. The burden of expenditure cuts fell on the most vulnerable members of the community. The most callous of those measures was the Gillard government's decision to slash the benefits of single mothers. The policy was supposed to encourage them to move from welfare to work, but it did not achieve its goal because unemployment was rising at the time. In the end, thousands of single mothers had their disposable income reduced by more than $100 per week and for no good cause, because the budget was still in deficit.

It was Labor's misfortune to be on the other side of the revenue boom – the bust. Every time the budget was updated, the deficit blew out. But Labor had already spent the forecast revenue before it was received, repeating the Coalition's mistake of assuming the windfalls would be permanent.

John Howard remains unrepentant. You'd expect nothing less. He is like Keating with the recession. These were the tax cuts we had to have, and he presents them in the same way as a profitable company might a Christmas bonus for its workforce, or a dividend for its shareholders. "There is a thing called the money belonging to the public and if the country is doing well, why can't the taxpayer have some of that money back," he says. "That was our view – and it was a view right across the government. I mean, there may have been individual arguments about the extent of this or that decision, but there was no serious dispute, I can tell you, inside the government about the desirability of giving tax cuts. And I don't also remember tremendous resistance from within the bureaucracy about the idea of giving tax cuts. There seemed to be a general acceptance.

You provide for defence; you provide for the essentials for the not-so-well-off; you provide for the Future Fund; you have a surplus of at least 1 per cent of GDP; and the rest, frankly, should be given back in tax cuts."

Leave to one side for now the question of whether that money should have been reinvested in infrastructure, or used to provide better government services, and ponder what the taxpayers did when they got their money back. They spent most of it, of course. But they wanted something else, and threw out the government despite its apparent generosity. It was clear by 2006 that the tax cuts were not helping the government in the electorate, but that only made Howard more determined to provide another round of them, and then another.

The Liberal Party pollster and strategist Mark Textor says Howard sacrificed his image as a resolute leader when he went on that spending spree between 2004 and 2007. "It was lazy money," he says. The public reaction was, "'Ok, anyone can throw money at things and frankly if I want a government to throw money at things, Labor does that better than the Liberals. So if it's really now about throwing money at things, I'll vote Labor.'"

There were other, more important reasons why Howard lost office in 2007. His breach of faith on WorkChoices was the most decisive issue.

"They saw him being opportunistic," Textor explains, "taking the opportunity that a majority in the lower and the upper house presented to sneak in a set of reforms for which there was no mandate and they thought, 'What's this about? I don't see the national good in this [and] I'm a little bit suspicious about why it was introduced.'"

But the cost of neglecting fiscal policy is the big lesson to be drawn from this era. Howard changed the budget from being a document primarily concerned with the economy to one with a purpose that was overtly political. He taught people to expect a handout outside an election campaign, which created a permanent sense of entitlement. The targeting was so obvious that the media could almost guess which section of the community would be next in line. His successors fell into the same habit, even though the budget was in deficit. Kevin Rudd increased the age pension in the 2009 budget after grey voters complained they had missed out the year before. Tony Abbott tried to buy the women's vote with a paid parental leave scheme that even Howard thought was too generous. With each futile attempt to bribe, government wasted another opportunity to reconsider the role of the budget in the twenty-first century. The public has had the more economically rational view on this issue for some time now. They want the government to stop throwing money at them and spend it instead on infrastructure. Although the first phase of the mining boom was the time to make those investments, it is still possible to do so with the budget in deficit. The key is to borrow while global interest rates remain at their lowest levels in about 500 years. Surely our federal and state governments can identify projects that generate a return to the economy above the cost of the loan. The budget need not blow out. Only the interest bill from new loans is counted in the bottom line, and that cost could be funded with a small tax rise, perhaps an increase in the Medicare levy.

There would be understandable political queasiness about taking such a step. Debt has been a dirty word since the Whitlam and Fraser deficits. But Australia remains an anomaly of globalisation: a nation that can afford to borrow more. The federal government debt, which is the sum of the budget deficits since 2008, is expected to peak at 18 per cent of gross domestic product this year, before falling. In Europe, government debts of 100 per cent or more of GDP are commonplace.

The obvious danger is that politics uses infrastructure as an excuse to leave the budget in deficit. Yet the borrowing would be more credible to the electorate, and to the financial markets, if the budget was returned to surplus. It would, in fact, signal a new form of discipline, as governments moved from vote-buying to nation-building.

***

In all of this, neither side has been prepared to confront the structure of the budget. They crab-walk around the revenue side of the problem, and take indiscriminate nips at the spending side.

The first budget after the global financial crisis forecast a recession for Australia, with unemployment peaking at more than 8 per cent. When the recession did not come, Treasury told the government that a small surplus could be achieved in 2012–13. Wayne Swan stuck to that deadline in his next three budgets, thus elevating a forecast into an iron-clad commitment. When he finally gave up the quest at the end of 2012, the goal of surplus had been pushed back to 2015–16. So much political pain could have been avoided if Treasury had stuck to its original pessimistic forecast.

If Tony Abbott and Joe Hockey had been doing their sums in opposition, they might have encouraged Labor to cut harder and to broaden the tax base, so that they would inherit a budget on the right trajectory. But they were having too much fun shouting down every Labor proposal to tighten the budget. That's politics, perhaps, and they'd happily plead guilty to the charge of pulling down the government. But they also promised to fix the budget with a formula that never made sense given the deficit they knew they would inherit. Abbott, in particular, somehow thought he could charm the budget into surplus while reducing taxes and increasing spending.

Joe Hockey's first budget, in 2014, pushed back a surplus to 2018–19. In the following year, he said we would have to wait till 2019–20. At the mid-year update in December 2015, the new treasurer, Scott Morrison, placed his opening bid for surplus at 2020–21.

The most telling article written after Abbott's demise was by Dennis Atkins of the *Courier-Mail.* It revealed a proposal put to cabinet, a fortnight before Abbott's dismissal, to scrap one of his government's own taxes. Originally a Labor idea, the $500 million deposit levy on the banks was a form of insurance in case one of them needed to be bailed out in the future. The measure had been announced in Hockey's second budget, and was due to take effect in January 2016.

"Hockey, who was desperate to get as much money as he could to drive down the deficit, wanted that $500 million but Abbott saw it as an easy way to attack Labor's Bill Shorten," Atkins wrote.

One of the leading opponents of scrapping the tax at that meeting was Malcolm Turnbull, who said it was simply an insurance levy such as many businesses incur when dealing with large amounts of money.

Abbott brushed off these objections, saying it was a good way to brand Shorten as a "bank bandit" who always looked to raising taxes.

Turnbull later told colleagues the government had "thrown away half a billion a year for a press release."

Abbott was certainly not the first prime minister to see the budget as a plaything of politics. But it was unusual to attack your own deficit-reduction measure for the sake of a slogan. In Abbott's binary view of the budget, taxes were evil and government defined itself by the voters it gave money to.

If Turnbull is to reset the budget debate, he has to abandon the Liberal mantra that taxes must always be cut. Both sides of the budget have to be deployed in the search for fairness and efficiency, and in the present climate that means an active search for ways to unwind the Howard Gift without crashing the economy. The most obvious target for Turnbull was the tax concessions for superannuation. He took his best shot ahead of the 2016 election, and almost started a civil war within the Coalition. The package was watered down after the election to placate higher income earners in the city and in the bush. It was barely worth the controversy. The promised saving to the budget was modest to begin with – $3.1 billion over four years. The compromise will yield a saving of just $2.8 billion. While the argued with itself, the deficit blew out again. Each opportunity lost will reduce our options in the next global shock, when the budget will be called on to stimulate the economy again.

A Recession We Have to Have?

It's time for a refresher course on the meaning of recession, because Australia has entered the danger zone where history warns that one is coming. Two threats in particular are coalescing, one local and one international. The property market is overheated in Sydney, and to a lesser extent in Melbourne. And the global economy is facing its third serious downturn in nine years. Our open economic model has shown it can cope with either one of these risks, but we don't know if it can handle both together.

The past offers little comfort, because the moments of Australia's greatest economic vulnerability come when soaring house prices combine with a global shock. If the worst comes to pass and China joins the United States and Europe as victims of capitalism's extended crisis, a recession of some kind will be difficult to avoid.

The housing bubble is the economist's version of Gallipoli, a nation-scarring event which destroys a generation. Our first global humiliation had its source in the Melbourne and Sydney land busts of the 1890s, which ended our long colonial reign as the world's richest people. Property prices collapsed by 50 per cent and 25 per cent respectively, banks closed their doors and unemployment jumped to double digits and remained there for a decade. The Australian economy took twenty years to recover the loss of income from that depression. The Keating recession of 1990–91 contained every one of those maladies: a housing boom and bust; the failure of state banks, building societies and credit unions; and unemployment remaining above 10 per cent for a number of years. Property prices didn't fall by as much, but they did stagnate for the remainder of the 1990s.

Although the IMF thinks our economy will keep growing, it sees property as the biggest domestic threat: "A sharp correction in house prices, possibly driven by Sydney, could be triggered by external conditions ... or a domestic shock to employment. This might have wider ramifications if it affects confidence."

Furthermore, "Over half of Australia's exports go to emerging Asia and nearly two thirds are non-rural commodity exports. An unexpectedly sharp fall in iron ore prices could reduce prices below production costs, and further dent incomes and growth. It would also likely dent foreign investment in Australian property and other markets, adversely affecting prices."

Hooked on capital gain and reliant on the trade of one big country: this is the familiar face of Australian smugness. But it is more than that. This particular housing boom, which began in 2012, defies the old rule that prices only climb at times of reckless confidence in the future. The economy has been soft, and our politics dysfunctional. Neither would seem to warrant another splurge on housing. Yet our two most globalised cities are behaving as if the party will never stop. The explanation is not merely economic, but cultural. Australians now see property as a shield against globalisation. Fear, not greed, has been driving up prices. This is an unprecedented development, which is drawing us ever closer to the crisis we thought we had side-stepped in 2008–09.

The Reserve Bank has been powerless to stop this latest spike in property prices because interest rates no longer work the way the open economic model intended. To understand why, it is worth recalling the last occasion that Sydney menaced the national economy. It was the giddy period between 2001 and 2003, when politics and the media competed to talk up the property market. John Howard had doubled the first home owner's grant, *Kath & Kim* hit our television screens, and households were spending more in total than they earned.

"I thought we were very close to having a bubble," the bank's governor at the time, Ian Macfarlane, says. "We had house prices going up by 20 per cent per annum; we had lending for housing going up by 20-plus per cent per annum. We had nearly half of it going into speculative investment housing. We had all these spruikers going around telling you how to get rich quick and, as someone pointed out to me ... we had something like seven programs on prime-time television telling you how to get rich quick through property development. So you put all those things together [and] it sounds like you're getting very close to a bubble."

Sydney house prices had run so far ahead of the rest of the nation that by the end of 2003 they were 40 per cent above Melbourne's and Brisbane's and 50 per cent above Perth's.

Macfarlane says: "We put a lot of thought into understanding what was happening and what we saw we didn't like very much. Fortunately, we had other reasons as well to raise interest rates. So we raised interest rates twice in 2002 and again twice in 2003."

In the end, house prices didn't collapse. "If they had've collapsed, that would have proved that it was a bubble. But they flattened right out, and there was very little growth for the next two or three years. In fact, in Sydney they fell, because Sydney was the hottest market. We got through that, I think, in reasonable shape, although we're always going to be worried from time to time about house prices in Australia. It's part of the landscape."

Howard wasn't happy. As he approached the 2004 election, he found voters concerned about interest rates. He framed the campaign as a question of trust: who would you trust to keep rates low, him or Mark Latham? And he began showering voters with cash. The baby bonus and a record boost to family payments were the down-payment. After the election, the money kept pouring onto the kitchen table. As mentioned, each budget of Howard's final term contained a tax cut larger than its predecessor's. Once again, the Reserve Bank was able to reduce the risk of inflation by countering the tax cuts with higher interest rates.

An unintended benefit of this was that Australia had a larger buffer than other rich nations when the global financial crisis hit. Rates could therefore be cut often and quickly to restore consumer and business confidence. The US Federal Reserve, by contrast, had slashed interest rates before the financial meltdown of September 2008. By Christmas, the US official rate was zero and it would remain there for the next seven years. Another advantage not widely appreciated at the time was that Sydney did not get ahead of itself during the first or second phases of the mining boom. House prices were essentially flat between 2004 and 2011, which meant the city most likely to import the contagion of speculation that infected the US and European property markets did no harm. With Sydney in remission, the banks were able to take their business to the rest of the country. Melbourne and Perth prices came within 10 per cent of Sydney's, and Brisbane within 20 per cent. Although housing was now less affordable across the continent, the important thing was that prices did not overshoot because the Reserve Bank was able to keep lifting interest rates throughout the boom. Also, our banks were well regulated and, unlike their counterparts in the United

States, did not lend recklessly. The open model was at its best in those years.

Soon after the emergency cuts of the global financial crisis, the Reserve Bank wanted to raise interest rates to more normal levels, and for a while it seemed it would have its way, because we were riding the back-to-back recovery waves of the Rudd–Gillard stimulus program and the second mining boom. But then interest rates had to be slashed again, as the eye of capitalism's storm reached Europe and the mining boom peaked. This was the period when the open model lost its flexibility. Australian interest rates were cut twelve times between November 2011 and August 2016, to a new record low of 1.5 per cent.

Inevitably, these reductions awakened the demon of the Sydney property market. House prices in Sydney have surged by 64 per cent between 2011 and 2016. Apartment prices jumped by 50 per cent. In the next hottest market, Melbourne, house prices rose by 37 per cent and apartments by 15 per cent. The Reserve Bank could not respond with higher interest rates as it did before, because the rest of the economy was weak. Victoria, Queensland and South Australia have each been close to recession on a couple of occasions since 2011. Western Australia is coming off the high of the mining boom, while Tasmania has already suffered a recession.

Without the interest-rate lever to pull, authorities have encouraged banks to restrict lending to investors. But this is a second-best option. Sydney is almost back where it was in 2003, a third more expensive than Melbourne and 40 per cent more expensive than Perth and Brisbane. The IMF says Sydney is one of the most expensive markets in the world and Australian housing is overvalued by about 10 per cent. If prices were to fall even by half that amount, it could be the psychological trigger for a recession. The Reserve Bank has left itself just enough room to reduce interest rates again in the event of another crisis. But it can't go much lower before we join the rest of the world in the quicksand of a zero official interest rate, from which no rich nation has yet been able to launch a sustainable recovery.

THE RISE, FALL AND RISE OF THE SYDNEY PROPERTY MARKET

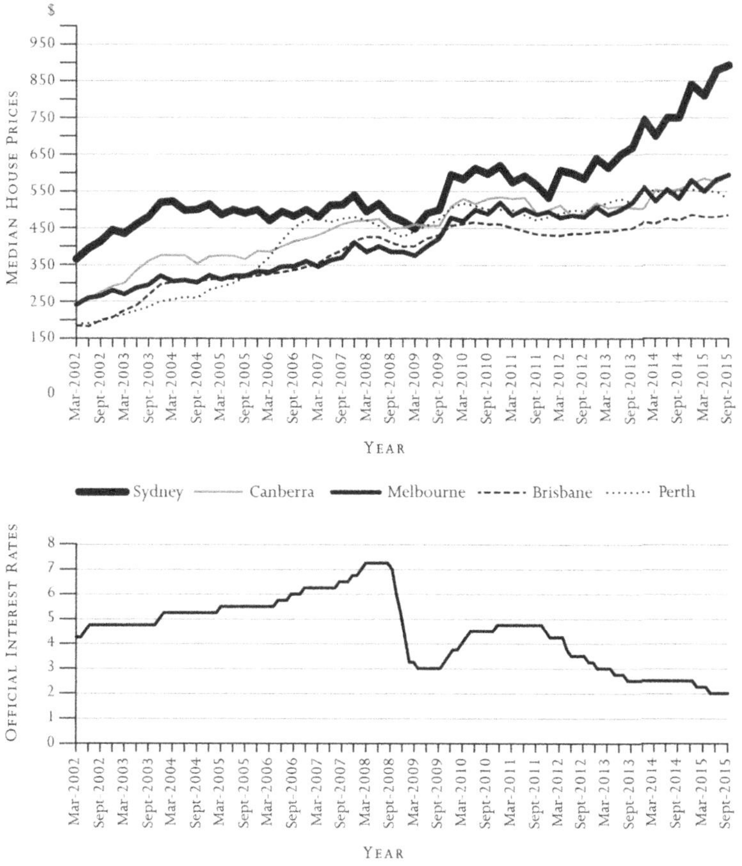

On top of the list of national regrets if we do fall into recession this year or next will be the role that politics played in fostering our property obsession. Every prime minister and treasurer since Hawke and Keating has indulged it with tax concessions. Keating did try to include housing in his program to modernise the economy. When he abolished negative gearing for investment properties in 1985, he said it was "an outrageous rort" which was holding back investment in more productive areas of the economy.

The outrageous rort was restored two years later, and for the simplest political reason. The Sydney property market had cooled, and Keating wanted to revive it ahead of the NSW state election in 1988. He didn't save the Labor government, but he did bring the speculators back, and prices have been edging further out of reach of first-time buyers ever since.

The landlord class in Australia – the number of people owning more than one property – numbered 600,000 in 1998–99. A decade later, their ranks had doubled to 1.275 million, or almost 13 per cent of individuals. John Howard gave the investor another leg up by halving the capital gains tax rate in 1999. That was the last year our landlord class declared a profit. Between 2000–01 and 2012–13, the most recent year for which statistics are available, our landlord class lost $66.3 billion, or $5.1 billion per year, more than they made in rental income. I'm pulling your leg. They didn't lose this money. Their fellow taxpayers did, because the landlords wrote off the losses against other income, thereby reducing the total tax they paid.

On the latest count, Australia has 1.9 million property investors, comprising 15 per cent of all taxpayers. They prefer to invest in existing properties, thus inflating prices without adding to the stock of housing. In any normal market, higher prices would encourage new entrants to increase the supply. But property is the blind spot of the open model – a corrupted market created with the blessing of politics.

This time-bomb is not easily defused. The best opportunity to curtail negative gearing was during the global financial crisis, but the Rudd government did not seriously consider it. Only now, in Opposition, is Labor prepared to address the mistake Keating made three decades ago. It wants to abolish negative gearing for those who buy existing properties. The question is whether it is already too late to reduce the threat of a bust.

One of the most concerning aspects of the housing boom since 2011 is the resumption of the debt cycle. Australian households owe more now than they did before the global financial crisis. Let that thought sink in. Record low interest rates did not encourage us to repay existing loans quicker. After a few years of belt-tightening, we returned to the bad habits of the Howard era.

Household debt peaked at 172 per cent of disposable income in mid-2007. By the end of 2011, it had been reduced to 167 per cent, still high by world standards but pointing in the right direction – down. The latest figure is 187 per cent. More than half the increase of the past five years is explained by the landlord class. If there is a recession, this is the group that will be kicking itself for borrowing too much.

Even if we stage another great escape and the economy keeps growing into the next decade, the open model has demonstrated its limitations. The inability to contain the Sydney property market reminds us that interest rates are an inherently blunt weapon. They can't control a boom once it is underway.

***

Recessions are notoriously tricky to predict, and even harder to define. Politicians and the media rely on the formula coined by Paul Keating in 1990: an economy that contracts for two quarters in a row. It is an arbitrary standard. For example, GDP could fall by 0.1 per cent and 0.1 per cent in consecutive quarters and that would be a recession. But if it collapsed by 1 per cent in one quarter and grew by 0.1 per cent the next, presumably it wasn't.

"If the Australian economy has a couple of quarters of negative growth, where instead of growing by three quarters of a percentage point it goes backward by 0.1 or something, does that really matter?" Ken Henry asks. "Politically that matters a lot. But does it really matter? Well, it probably doesn't matter a hell of a lot to Australia. But if it's a recession that gives us 10 per cent unemployment, then we really should be worried. We should do whatever we can to avoid that. [More than half] the people aged over forty-five who lost their jobs in the early 1990s recession never worked a day again in their lives. That is a consequence that should be avoided not at any cost, but at any reasonable cost."

The unemployment rate is the key to distinguishing the deep recessions from the shallow ones. Once it starts climbing, it is already too late to prevent a hard landing. The Keating recession cast a shadow over the entire 1990s and it wasn't until 2003 that the unemployment rate returned to its pre-recessionary low.

The reason the rest of the world still envies us is that our unemployment rate was contained during the global financial crisis. It did not cross 6 per cent during the crisis, which meant it could be quickly brought back below 5 per cent in the recovery.

As the economist John Quiggin pointed out, the initial success of the Rudd government's stimulus program meant Australia also avoided the next trap in the crisis, "the swing to extreme austerity that characterised most of the developed world."

> Even Abbott and Hockey, despite talking up a debt and deficit crisis, shied away from really serious austerity measures. The results speak for themselves, particularly in the job market. Australia's employment–population ratio was barely affected by the global financial crisis. In Britain, the United States, Ireland and Canada, employment fell sharply ... and has never recovered.

But our unemployment rate has been drifting higher since mid-2011, and almost every economic advantage we enjoyed before the global financial crisis has either diminished or disappeared. The interest-rate buffer is almost gone; the budget is in deficit; households are deeper in debt; house prices are inflated; and China cannot come to the rescue again.

The next global shock, whenever it comes, will find us with our economic guard down, and a political system that has shredded its authority.

Reconstruction

Any system, be it political, economic or environmental, must adapt to maintain stability. Otherwise, the system risks collapse. In the past, Australian complacency would be broken by an economic crisis, which would trigger a political crisis. Stability would only be restored after politics designed a new economic model. The cycles of recession and renewal have been inverted in the twenty-first century, with a political crisis preceding an economic crisis. It has been twenty-five years since our last deep recession, yet in the past five years we have had as many prime ministers as Greece.

Politics has brought this crisis on itself by underestimating the public. Mark Textor says voters have grasped the meaning of the open model and are ruthlessly applying its lessons at the ballot box.

> Before the '80s, government guaranteed a lot of things. They guaranteed a pension for life, they guaranteed certain Australian industries. People understood that was changing, but they also understood that when that changed they should guarantee less [in return]. If you want me to live in an economy where I can trade and work with whoever I want – if you are offering me less loyalty as a government – I can offer you less loyalty as a voter.

Australians fired their first warning shot at the 1990 election, when they gave the main parties their lowest combined primary vote in almost fifty years. Support for the minor parties was 17.4 per cent, and Labor became the first government to be re-elected with a primary vote below 40 per cent.

It was a harbinger. At the *Tampa* election of 2001, the hung parliament of 2010 and Tony Abbott's victory in 2013, the minor-party vote was even higher than in 1990. The 2013 election damned both sides. Labor suffered its lowest primary vote since the Great Depression, while the Coalition's primary was the lowest for an incoming conservative government in Australian history. The structural decline in the base vote of the main parties has undermined the policy-making process. Governments live in dread of losing power after a single term, and so they churn through announcements in a pitiful search for approval in the polls. Oppositions understand the fear of the incumbent, because they lived with it only a few years earlier. They obstruct because they know it's the simplest way back into office. Politics has casualised its own employment market, making every position in the system temporary. Malcom Turnbull had almost six years in the wilderness to observe both our domestic political crisis and the global economic crisis. The time between losing the Opposition leadership in December 2009 and seizing the prime ministership in September 2015 is the political equivalent of an older worker retraining for a new career. Both sides of politics have compelling redemption stories that could have encouraged Turnbull, in which broken or divisive men used their second chance to change the country and restore confidence in the system. John Curtin and Bob Hawke gave up the grog before Labor could trust them with the leadership. Robert Menzies and John Howard came back as conservative leaders who could relate to the people. The catch for Turnbull is that he has to be both Curtin and Menzies, and Hawke and Howard, to succeed. He has to author a new model and run a long-term government. The former is a precondition for the latter, but his first full year in office was not encouraging.

If he had a new model, we should be able to recite it by now. Instead, we witnessed an aimless debate on the GST, and an election campaign based on a slogan: "jobs and growth." What has been missing so far is an explanation of the economic problems Turnbull wants to solve. He can't do this until he removes the blinkers of ideology and nostalgia from his side of politics in the way Curtin and Hawke once did for Labor.

The Coalition can't lay claim to the future until it adjusts to the two big shocks of our age. The first shock is that the version of capitalism favoured by conservatives is broken. The crisis entered its ninth year in 2016, which places it in the same category as the global depressions of the 1890s and 1930s. The epicentre has shifted from the American housing market and Wall Street to Europe. Now it threatens

China, the nation most likely to end Australia's long economic winning streak. The crisis won't pass until capitalism finds a new source of market-based growth. Until then, as the IMF and others have been saying for some years, governments must step in to fill the void. Not as temporary support for their economies, but to fix the things that are holding back recovery, most notably public infrastructure. Turnbull is to the right of most Australians on economics, and a little to their left on social policy. He has faith in markets and multiculturalism. However, fate has dealt him the responsibility of renewing the open model by going against his own instincts for smaller government.

The second shock is that the international community may finally be ready to tackle climate change. This should be Turnbull's vindication: the times finally suit the call he made in 2009 for a market-based response. But the price he paid for removing Tony Abbott was the retention of the former prime minister's compromised policy, which relies on government spending to reduce greenhouse-gas emissions. It cannot work without tearing an even larger hole in the budget. In its first full year of operation, 2014–15, Direct Action saw emissions rise, reversing gains made under Labor's carbon tax.

And then there is the ever-present danger of another economic setback.

***

Most high-income nations would still love to have our problems. Australia is one of the few advanced economies with demography on its side. We have not yet hit the speed hump of ageing. Our open economic model remains the gold standard. But politics is killing our future because the open model can't manage the transition anymore. The Sydney property market has seen to that. The open model was supposed to ensure stability by removing four key prices in the economy from political control: the currency, interest rates, tariffs and wages. The job of steering the economy passed from government to the invisible hand of the market. If the economy went off-course, the Reserve Bank was there to guide it back to safer waters. Governments forgot that markets and central banks can fail just as spectacularly as interventionist politicians.

Australia remains unnecessarily exposed to the extended crisis in capitalism because our leaders stopped thinking. They behave as if a better system will fall out of the sky and relieve us of the responsibility of making our own future.

Today the world has no better system for us to choose, because every version of capitalism is under attack. The United States, Europe and China account for more than half the world's total production. Each has a readily identifiable model. The Americans have the freest markets, the Europeans the most comprehensive welfare system, and the Chinese the most active government sector. None can say their particular phase of the crisis is behind them. None can point to a better model. They serve only as warnings for Australia of the policies that don't work.

The disruptions we associate with the twenty-first century have a long tail winding back to the 1980s. They are an inescapable part of globalisation, generating income and instability in almost equal measure. The United States carried the global economy in the 1980s and '90s, even as its innovations in finance and technology undermined it. China has been underwriting it since 2007, even though its savings glut helped precipitate the global financial crisis. Within Europe, Germany serves the same conflicting role as growth engine and unforgiving banker.

The shifts in global economic power are more nuanced than the easy headline of Asia rising at the expense of the North Atlantic. The first fifteen years of the Asian century have witnessed a boom and a bust in Europe, a long stagnation in the United States, and the extraordinary growth in China cancelling an almost equivalent loss in Japan. Europe, not China, accounted for the largest share of global growth between 2000 and 2007 and almost caught the United States in total size before it was overwhelmed by the global financial crisis.

China was responsible for just over a third of total world growth over the next seven years. By 2014, the United States accounted for 22.5 per cent of the global economy, the Euro area was a much diminished

17.4 per cent, while China reached 13.4 per cent. The test of the Chinese model is whether it consolidates those gains, or suffers a severe correction like the Europeans.

Intriguingly, China's share of the global economy today is almost identical to Japan's in 2000. Japan was fading long before the Asian century for reasons that should terrify the Europeans today, and perhaps even the Chinese. Japan's financial system never recovered from its property bubble in the late 1980s, and now, as its population ages, new sources of dynamism are hard to find. The Chinese appreciate this danger, and have taken steps to inspire a new baby boom by abandoning their one-child policy. But the conundrum has not changed: will they grow old before they become rich?

The sequencing of the crisis, from the United States to Europe and now China, suggests that the American economy should drive global growth in the next few years. It had begun to do so at the end of Barack Obama's presidency. Whether Donald Trump changes this trajectory remains to be seen. Either way, the US is unlikely to regain the swagger it had in the 1980s and '90s.

The young working men and women of the Reagan era have reached middle age and they are not coping with change. A troubling spike in deaths by drug poisoning, suicide and chronic liver disease has increased the mortality rate for those aged forty-five to fifty-four. This is unusual in a high-income society, and a vivid illustration of the human cost of a free-market society without an adequate safety net. Research by Princeton University's Anne Case and Angus Deaton compared midlife mortality rates between 1999 and 2013 in the United States and six other rich nations, including Australia. Only the US showed an increase in deaths per 100,000 people, an extraordinary finding on its own. But when Case and Deaton broke down mortality rates among white, black and Hispanic Americans, they found only white Americans were affected by this scourge. (Mortality rates fell sharply for both black and Hispanic Americans.) The researchers said "the epidemic of pain, suicide, and drug overdoses" may be tied to loss of economic security and widening income inequality since the 1970s. "Many of the baby-boom generation are the first to find, in midlife, that they will not be better off than were their parents. Growth in real median earnings has been slow for this group, especially those with only a high school education."

Politicians here might shrug and say that this doesn't apply to Australia, because we recorded the second-lowest death rate for middle-aged men and women after Sweden. We don't have the American problem of a white underclass. But we do have a prosperity gap between new Australians and the local-born. The post-war assumption that migrants to Australia will only do the work that the locals don't want no longer applies. Now migrants are also being hired for work that the locals are not qualified for. Professor Bob Gregory has found that migrants account for virtually all the full-time jobs created in Australia since 2007. They didn't displace the local-born; they just took the cream of the new positions on offer, most notably in the professions. Our "extraordinary economic success since the global financial crisis owes a great deal to the increased level of national income" generated by these latest arrivals, Gregory concluded. "Mining booms come and go, but large population changes last forever."

On the other hand, the success of the migrant raises the risk of a local backlash, and the possibility that one of our main parties will take a detour down the American road of bigotry. If the political system couldn't cope with the infrastructure demands of the past decade, how will it respond to a future in which a fraction of the local-born feel that they have been pushed to the margins of society? The logical answer is to dramatically increase public investment in education to ensure these local-born are not left behind. But this would require a change of mindset in the Coalition, which supports private systems over public, and the winners of deregulation over the losers.

The onus on government is to repair the social contract before inequality becomes entrenched. Malcolm Turnbull does seem to understand this need. He said he wants Australia to remain a high-wage society with a generous social safety net. Yet something doesn't add up. He also presents as a leader who wants to cut taxes further and shrink the size of government. The experience of the twenty-first century so far tells us these ideas are not compatible.

The tax cuts of the boom years, which favoured higher income earners, and the spending cuts since the global financial crisis, which punished those at the bottom, overturned a century of political tradition to promote egalitarianism through the federal budget. Turnbull can't improve the open model by repeating the formula which alienated the electorate in the first place.

The political dialogue about tax has to change. This is an argument conservatives can make in the twenty-first century if they are prepared to learn from the example of Labor in the 1980s. Hawke and Keating inherited a budget with a spending problem, and badly designed taxes. They cut spending and simplified the tax system, but did not reduce overall revenue. They explained to the public that they were correcting for the spending errors of the Whitlam era, and Labor supporters accepted the argument. Turnbull can do the same on the revenue side by explaining the budget policy mistakes of the Howard era. Too much money was given to those who didn't need it, and too little of it was put aside for the future.

Politicians mistake the trade-offs of deregulation for immutable laws, when in fact they are choices made by politicians, whether actively or by neglect. Deregulation need not have increased household debt to the extent that it has, nor led to a greater concentration of national wealth in the property market. These are not rational outcomes of a free market, but the result of political decisions to favour one form of investment over all others. Governments used financial deregulation to create the illusion of sound economic management. They boasted budget surpluses, while encouraging households to take on debt.

The danger was not sufficiently appreciated during the long credit boom. Economies were strong, and governments could look forward to re-election. Once the global financial crisis hit, households returned to their pre-deregulation levels of thrift. That rational switch from borrower to saver has undermined capitalism ever since, even in Australia, because markets cannot thrive without confident consumers.

Having come through the global financial crisis so well, Australia should have been able to shift some of the risk back onto the government balance sheet without European-style levels of public debt. I know every second politician has screamed about debt and deficit, but this is one of the most necessary steps in the transition. Households will not be assured about the future until they get on top of their own debts, and see the government taking more responsibility in areas such as infrastructure.

To date, the shortcut of populism is more appealing than the intellectual ordeal of adapting the open model for the twenty-first century. Labor had a reasonable expectation of returning to government in 2016 if Tony Abbott was prime minister. If so, it would have been the first federal Labor Opposition to be elected on the basis of a protest vote. Instead, it hoped that the loss wouldn't be devastating. The election, and the future, was Malcolm Turnbull's to lose.

The test Turnbull has set for himself, and the community, is to exploit the transition to Australia's advantage. The nation is smarter than its politicians have given it credit for. The workforce already reflects that in the rise of the professional. Turnbull should use his greatest electoral asset – his intelligence – to argue for a smarter nation. While we will never be big enough to play the market-rigging games of the Americans, Chinese or Germans, we do have something they crave: potential. It may be hard to believe after a quarter of a century of uninterrupted growth, but Australia is still developing. We remain an anomaly among high-income nations, a small population in charge of a resource-rich continent. While our natural advantage in coal and iron ore risks turning to curse now that the minerals cycle has turned, we still have a country to which people want to migrate.

The global financial crisis is forcing every nation to re-examine the role of government. High-income nations are investing more in physical infrastructure, education and innovation. They are doing so to prop up their economies in crisis. Australia can intervene from a position of relative strength. What is missing at the moment is genuine political insight. The challenge for government in the twenty-first century is to think for the long term. Planning is the simplest political concept, but it goes against every instinct of the contemporary leader. Part of the problem is that the main parties are stuck in the wrong past: they keep looking to the market to fix problems that can only be solved by government. Both the conservatives and Labor need to give Howard, Keating and Hawke a break and look instead to the post-war reconstruction of Curtin, Chifley and Menzies for inspiration. If Australia is to stay ahead of the pack, it needs governments that understand markets well enough to know where government belongs. Otherwise, Australia will become globalisation's next and most unnecessary victim.

The one thing weighing us down is the chip on our shoulder. In the past, we only found inspiration after the fall. It took the Great Depression and World War II to provide the energy and focus for the reconstruction that laid the foundation for modern Australia. Will we have to wait for another crash before we find the model that restores stability to our twenty-first century?

Afterword

AUSTRALIA DIVIDED

Malcolm Turnbull can divide the seismic political year of 2016 into halves of indecision. The first six months were lost in a fruitless search for an agenda, the last six months were spent watching his back.

The defining event of the prime minister's year, and ours, was the election count on the evening of 2 July. It was probably Turnbull's last meaningful chance to persuade the public that he could lift the curse of the Rudd–Gillard–Abbott era. Unable to claim victory on the night, he could have used his time at the lectern to project a humble authority. To assume his government would be returned with a working majority, but accept that he had disappointed voters. If he had found the rhetorical sweet spot between confidence and contrition, the nation might have gone to bed that night with an open mind.

Instead, he closed it with a flash of entitled anger that is not easily forgotten. Turnbull protested that Labor had run "some of the most systematic, well-funded lies ever peddled in Australia." The text message to voters on the morning of the election, warning that the Coalition would privatise Medicare, was tricked up to look as if Medicare itself had sent it. "No doubt the police will investigate," Turnbull bellowed. "But this is the scale of the challenge we faced. And regrettably more than a few people were misled."

A crooked opponent and a rigged election. This was Donald Trump's complaint whenever he fell behind Hillary Clinton in the opinion polls.

Obviously, Turnbull is no Trump. He is neither buffoon nor demagogue. But on the night of the election, Turnbull channelled Trump in one surprising respect. He couldn't see past the Liberals in the room to the other side of the television camera, where Australians of all colours, from the partisan to the apathetic, were watching. At one point in his war cry, Turnbull even uttered a banality that recalled the manic sloganeering of Abbott. The Coalition stood for "the values of freedom, of business, of enterprise and entrepreneurship," he said. Labor's alternative was "more debt, more deficit and higher taxes."

But the conservative base wasn't persuaded. Over the following days, MPs on the right took pot shots at Turnbull and his team for straying too far to the centre during the campaign.

Liberal senator Cory Bernardi put the critique this way: "You cannot turn your back on your party base, and this is something I've consistently warned about for many, many years. We had our chief pollster, Mark Textor, say that 'the base doesn't matter, they've got nowhere to go, we'll pick up more votes in the centre.' We had the prime minister, Malcolm Turnbull, say

Pauline Hanson has no place in Australian politics and yet she ... reflects the concerns of many, many people."

You see what he did. Bernardi defined the conservative base as the heart of the nation, and Hanson as a member of the political mainstream. Interestingly, he misquoted Textor in order to stretch the definition of the centre. Textor had said that far rightwing websites don't matter, a harmless observation in the Australian context. But to Bernardi, the blogger is the critical voter, the cyber vanguard of a conservative movement. This is a very American way of looking at the Australian electorate.

Yet the Bernardi formula has clearly been on Turnbull's mind. In the six months after the election, the prime minister was the very model of the uncompromising conservative his internal critics told him to be. He went after the trade unions, continued to play hardball with the refugees on Nauru and Manus Island despite the growing international condemnation, and ruled out any market-based mechanism to reduce carbon pollution. Yet still the conservatives whinged that he is not one of them. This is a very American way of looking at one's own side of politics. Every concession to the right encouraged a fresh demand. The goal wasn't to settle the dispute but to escalate it.

No Coalition government has been this conflicted since Malcolm Fraser's final term in 1980–83, when the incumbent wets and the insurgent dries engaged in open civil war on economic policy. That argument suited the times because the old protectionist model was broken, and it crossed party lines when the Hawke–Keating Labor government implemented much of the dry agenda.

The fault line running through the Coalition now has nothing to do with economic policy. It is cultural. Should gay couples have the right to marry? Should bigots have the right to say whatever they want?

Before he became prime minister, Turnbull answered an emphatic yes to the first question and a disinterested no to the second. He thought parliament was the forum to rule on marriage equality, and called out Abbott's proposal for a plebiscite to determine public opinion as a delaying tactic. He did not see why the government should waste time on the *Racial Discrimination Act.*

Turnbull reversed his position on the plebiscite to help swing conservatives in the leadership ballot against Abbott in 2015, and is now prepared to entertain changes to the *RDA.* Only a zealot could look at the *RDA* and think it is a pressing concern for Australians. Especially when the previous push for "reform" in 2014 ended in tears because there was virtually no public support for it. Yet the conservatives have talked about virtually nothing else since the election.

There is a maddening circularity to these debates. Politicians and activists enter them knowing they can't convince those on the opposing side to change their mind. If pressed, most will agree that these issues are a distraction from whatever the main game is. Yet the combatants willingly return to the field of obsession, for another nil-all draw. We are used to Labor being the party of tedious introspection. Now the virus of self-absorption has spread to the side of politics that was supposed to be the practical one.

The risk, acknowledged across the main parties, but never taken seriously enough to change their behaviour, is that they are undermining democracy through neglect. Every policy challenge avoided, every attempt to blame-shift to the other side, or to another tier of government, every insider indulgence from rorted travel expenses to factional warfare invites the backlash of populism.

The Australian electorate has already fractured. To see it, consider the nation as three economic and cultural zones.

The people most comfortable with globalisation in the Asian century live in the south-east corner: New South Wales, Victoria and the ACT. These states (and territory) generally pay their own way in the federation.

The people who are whiter than the nation are in the mining states of Queensland and Western Australia. Conservative-leaning, these states track the extremes of our national income, collecting the greatest windfall in the boom and suffering the hardest landing in the bust.

The people most dependent on government welfare are in the outsider belt of Tasmania, South Australia and the Northern Territory. This is ground zero for both white and indigenous disadvantage in Australia.

In the south-east corner, Labor was the majority party of the 2016 election, winning 44 of the 86 seats. The Coalition won 40, the Greens one and independents one.

In the outsider belt, Labor claimed 12 of the 18 seats, the Coalition just four and independents two.

If the election had been decided in these two zones, between the winners and losers of globalisation, Labor would be in power.

But the Turnbull government was returned because its vote held up in the mining states. The Coalition held 32 of the 46 seats, Labor had just 13 and the independents one.

This was the first time in history that a federal government had such a narrow geographical mandate, and the first time that the south-east corner did not decide who ruled the country.

Rather than betraying his right flank, as his critics claimed, Turnbull was saved by it. The result mirrored the 2010 election, when Julia Gillard's Labor government won a majority of seats in New South Wales, Victoria, South Australia and Tasmania, while the Tony Abbott–led Coalition dominated in Queensland and Western Australia.

Think about what this is really telling us about the national mood. In 2010 and again in 2016, voters were offered a choice between platitudes: moving forward versus stop the boats, jobs and growth versus Mediscare. With no one to inspire them, voters reverted to tribal type. The backlash narrative of Brexit and Trump did not fit here because the incumbent survived. The real echo with Britain and the United States was in the tribalism. London, Liverpool and Manchester voted to remain in the European Union; the rest of England voted to leave. The big American cities voted for Hillary Clinton, the rest of the United States voted for Donald Trump. Cosmopolitan versus conservative.

The promise of Turnbull when he replaced Abbott as prime minister in September 2015 was that he could unite conservative and cosmopolitan Australia. But he second-guessed himself into policy stasis, and lost the opportunity to build a genuine coalition across the continent.

His performance at the ballot box was actually worse than Gillard's in 2010, even though the parliament wasn't hung this time. Turnbull lost 14 seats in total, three more than Gillard, but survived because he entered the election with a larger buffer.

Gillard could govern for three years because the balance of power tilted leftwards in both chambers. The lower house Greens and independents who supported her minority government came from Labor states: Victoria, New South Wales and Tasmania. The Greens held sway in the Senate. It is easy to forget this detail. Gillard could legislate because she didn't have to negotiate twice. She began with a unity of purpose on her side that Turnbull would kill for. The big decisions of her government – the price on carbon, the National Disability Insurance Scheme, and reform of schools funding – did not split the Labor caucus between environmentalists and sceptics, between interventionists and free-marketers, between advocates for public and private systems. The minor parties had Gillard's back; their interests and hers aligned because neither wanted to see an early election.

Turnbull, by contrast, has to navigate the hornet's nest of his own party room and the viper pit of the Senate. Conservatives and cosmopolitans are butting heads within the government, while the Senate minor parties are in direct competition with the Coalition. Pauline Hanson threatens the government in its strongest states, Queensland and Western Australia, while Nick Xenophon and Jacqui Lambie circle in its two weakest states, South Australia and Tasmania.

Logic says that Turnbull, or whoever succeeds him in the event of another coup, can only jump this trap by pitching to where the majority of voters reside, in the south-east corner. If that is too much of a stretch for the conservatives, the government could look to the outsider belt.

But the catch 22 of a majority anchored in Queensland and Western Australia is that any attempt to broaden the base will be taken by conservatives as a declaration of culture war. The mining states are not used to compromise. They have traditionally seen themselves as separate from the rest of the nation, trapped in the extended adolescence of the pioneer settlement.

Queenslanders voted for Joh Bjelke-Petersen when South Australia had Don Dunstan as premier, and they stuck with Joh through Gough Whitlam and Malcolm Fraser and even the first five years of the Hawke government. Western Australians were still talking secession as recently as the 1970s. The sense of separation in the west is accentuated by the mining cycle. In the boom years, the state complained that it was subsidising the rest of the country. Now, in the bust, it cries poor and demands a handout. Western Australia had closed the last decade in the strongest financial position of any state. By 2016, it had the largest debt, at $20 billion, and that debt is forecast to reach $26 billion in 2018 before it stabilises.

The mining states gave Pauline Hanson her second coming in 2016. She won two Senate places in Queensland, another in Western Australia and a fourth in New South Wales.

The One Nation vote in the Senate repeated the pattern of the late 1990s and fell the further south one travelled down the east coast of Australia: 9.2

per cent in Queensland; 4.1 per cent in New South Wales and 1.8 per cent in Victoria. It spiked again in Western Australia at 4 per cent. Here's the twist: Hanson had little traction in the two poorest states. She polled 3 per cent in South Australia and just 2.6 per cent in Tasmania, where Jacqui Lambie trebled the Hanson vote with 8.3 per cent and the Greens almost quadrupled it with 11.2 per cent. And the Greens outpolled One Nation in every state bar Queensland.

Take the Bernardi formula to its logical conclusion, placing the Coalition and Hanson in the same column, and the Senate vote reaffirms the polarity between the mining states and the outsider belt. The conservative primary vote averaged 44.8 per cent in Queensland and Western Australia, and 35.3 per cent in South Australia and Tasmania. Note that the South Australian Senator Cory Bernardi is in the least likely state from which to launch a new conservative party.

This is a little-understood aspect of Australia's political character. The outsider belt has a more substantial democratic heritage than the mining states. The voters there are among the most strategic in the country, and for decades they have sent deal-makers to the upper house to bargain on their behalf. Xenophon and Lambie are cut from the same pragmatic cloth as Janine Haines and Brian Harradine. Long may the outsiders negotiate, because if the nation's two poorest states ever joined the Hanson insurgency it could take many years to bring them back to the political centre.

The lesson of 2016, from the United States, Britain and Europe, is that voters, once disengaged, can be easily reanimated to wreck the system. Australians are well into the disengaged phase. All it would take to tip them into a Brexit or Trump mindset, a white rage against globalisation, is a deep recession.

***

THE GRIM LEGACY OF 2010

To be fair to the Americans, the British and the Europeans, our politics has been as demoralising as theirs. Australia's leaders stepped into the abyss ahead of the others, and without the push of economic crisis. Tony Abbott seized power on a platform of macho vulgarity three years before Donald Trump. Julia Gillard campaigned in jargon six years before Hillary Clinton. Their successors share some of the worrying traits of Britain's insipid politicians. Malcolm Turnbull reminds us of former prime minister David Cameron, an intellect seemingly without political insight. Bill Shorten has been too close for comfort to Labor's former leader Ed Miliband, an adolescent numbers man.

Although to be equally fair to our leaders, they have been overwhelmed by forces common to all democratic systems, most notably the disruptions of technology, demography and globalisation. For Australia, the year of disillusion was 2010. Faith in our democracy went into freefall after Kevin Rudd abandoned his reform program to tackle climate change. At each election since, the minor party vote has surged, first at the expense of Labor and then the Coalition. The swing to the minor parties was 4 per cent in 2010; a further 1.7 per cent in 2013; and another 2.1 per cent in 2016. There is no precedent for this in the post-war era. At the past two elections, the combined minor party vote exceeded 20 per cent. The last time that happened was during the Depression elections of 1931 and 1934. Back then, Labor suffered a double split – its left flank rallied behind former NSW premier Jack Lang; its right, led by former Tasmanian premier Joe Lyons, joined the conservatives to form the United Australia Party. Labor hasn't collapsed in a formal sense this time, but its vote has. Around 10 per cent of its former base has moved leftward, to the Greens. The shift occurred in 2010, and to date Labor has been unable to pull those people back as primary voters.

If the ascent of the minor parties was merely the story of the Greens, then it would be in keeping with previous breakouts from one of the main parties – from Labor to the Democratic Labor Party in the 1950s and from the Liberals to the Australian Democrats in the 1970s. But the swings in 2013 and 2016 have been to the right; to the Palmer United Party and then to Pauline Hanson's One Nation. The threat of a formal split lies with the Coalition now.

The main parties seem unable to arrest their collective decline. Policy remains unduly defensive; the approach to politics needlessly aggressive. Too much weight is still given to opinion polls, long after their utility had expired. In this regard, Australia has proven to be a world leader. Our political system had surrendered to the polls by 2010. Yet the election result that year came as a total surprise to most players. Six years before Brexit and Trump, the Australian people stunned the main parties, and the media, by hanging the parliament. It was assumed, by both sides, that the messy example of Julia Gillard's minority government would dissuade voters from another indecisive election. But they did so again in 2016. The problem is the parties, not the electorate. Australia won't recover from its political depression until it breaks with the bad habits of 2010.

TRIVIAL PURSUIT

Leadership and the End of the Reform Era

Introduction

Elections are a form of peer-group pressure, in which leaders are bullied into being as small-minded as the public at its worst. Yet voters are not so stupid that they can't see their knees being jerked. In 2010 Julia Gillard and Tony Abbott broke the democratic contract with a campaign so awful that it begged a collective rebuke.

I hadn't seen anything like it in more than twenty years of covering national affairs. It was a flip of a coin who was the more annoying: the robotic prime minister or the relentlessly negative Opposition leader. I wanted to pen a resignation letter to my employer: "Dear Rupert, sorry, I can't pretend that this contest is worth reporting. Neither candidate deserves to win. Julia won't talk the country up; Tony keeps talking it down."

Two amiable and intelligent politicians had frozen, together. They delivered no memorable quotes, let alone policies – merely slogans that quickly became punchlines at their own expense: "moving forward" and "the real Julia" versus "stop the boats" and "end the waste."

The quick, and romantic, conclusion to draw is that the people willingly smashed the machine by choosing none of the above on 21 August. To borrow one of Kevin Rudd's better mantras, Australia declared that this reckless style of campaigning must stop. That may be true, but I wouldn't take the next step and assume that a hung parliament is the solution to a crisis of governance that has been a decade in the making.

Today there is a whiff of the conflict-ridden 1970s in the air. The main parties have nothing to offer their supporters beyond conspiracy theories about their opponents. Labor blames the media and a bloody-minded Opposition for the shrill tone to the national conversation. The Coalition points the bone back at Labor, which it accuses of being the worst government in history.

Business and organised labour have assumed the right of veto over policies they don't like, and they spend millions in advertising to make their point. News organisations engage in turf wars, most notably the ABC and the *Australian.* The media reflect and reinforce the malaise through the restless search for another scandal to fill the 24-hour news cycle.

The election year felt like one long domestic dispute. The row didn't end with Rudd's dumping as prime minister; it just took another screwy form as Gillard and Abbott competed for the right to shrink the nation. In no previous post-war campaign had both sides agreed to reduce the immigration intake regardless of the economic cycle. Ben Chifley and Robert Menzies would turn in their graves if they knew their political grandchildren could be so easily intimidated by public opinion.

The 2010 campaign was the sound of a nation needlessly fracturing. Each side of politics clung like a barnacle to its version of reality. It is rare for the main parties to talk themselves into opposite corners of a room. One or the other has usually had a strong enough sense of where the majority sits to lay claim to it. But Gillard and Abbott, and behind them their poll-obsessed teams, were so terrified of offending the disengaged that they forgot to inspire the voters who were paying attention.

The Australia that revealed itself at the ballot box on 21 August was split every which way. Between the mining states and the southern states. Between men and women. And between old and young. The criss-cross of moods sent two unmistakable messages. To the Liberal Party and its coalition partner, the Nationals – Australia still leans centre-left, even in the bush. To the Labor Party – you blew it.

Losing It

Australians elect Labor governments to change things. They never give them large majorities, but they reward them with successive terms if they can look after the heart as well as the hip pocket.

The contract between voters and Coalition governments is less demanding. Conservatives invariably take office in a landslide and hold power for long stretches, provided that they don't inflict a recession on middle-income earners or unsettle them with a broken election promise such as WorkChoices.

These differing expectations make for a double standard that Labor people revel in because it fits with the heroic notion that theirs is the party of progress. But it also means Labor cannot afford to run a do-nothing government because Australians will mark it more harshly than the Coalition when it fails to deliver reform.

The issue that triggered Labor's loss of face in 2010 was climate change. Kevin Rudd had presented it as our greatest moral and economic challenge. So when he shelved his emissions trading scheme (ETS) in April, without so much as a sit-down press conference to explain why, his personal approval rating collapsed. He followed the backdown on climate change with a fight over the taxation of mining. Rudd wanted to prove he still had vision and strength, but he picked an issue that was too complex to be digested in the time he had left before the election was due to be called. The so-called resource super profits tax clarified why our system had lost its ability to solve problems. The government dropped the tax on the community with no warning in the week before the May budget. The Opposition didn't pause to digest the merits of the tax because it saw a political opportunity in obstruction. The miners went to war with an advertising campaign that tested the limits of our democracy. The media, transfixed by the prospect that Rudd might lose his job, surrounded the combatants like the crowd at a schoolyard brawl, willing each side to keep punching.

Labor let Tony Abbott get into its head. The Coalition's campaigns against the emissions trading scheme and the mining tax assumed that households were one electricity bill away from bankruptcy. Party polling showed that Abbott had a point, but not the one Labor latched onto. Concerns over the cost of living were most acute in Queensland, where Labor had the most marginal seats on the line. But Labor's majority wasn't under threat until it ran away from its own values. The mining tax wasn't a significant vote-switcher in the end, but climate change was, because Julia Gillard finished on the same hesitant page as Rudd. Her poll ratings, and Labor's, began to slide again after she announced that she would consult a citizens' assembly before legislating to put a price on carbon pollution. Leadership and conviction were at issue once more.

Conservatives see the defeat of the ETS and the 2010 election result as important shifts in the national mood. They interpret the fall of the British Labour government and the mid-term elections in the United States as signs of an international swing back to the right. The ballot box tells a different story, because Australia still leans centre-left. The most relevant statistic is the combined primary vote of Labor and the Greens. On 21 August, it was 49.8 per cent, only 1.4 per cent below the record of 2007. The Coalition primary vote was 43.6 per cent.

Labor rises at the two extremes of our economic cycle: in wartime or recession, as it did with John Curtin's government in 1941 or Bob Hawke's in 1983; or at the top of a boom, as was the case with the doomed trio of James Scullin in 1929, Gough Whitlam in 1972 and Kevin Rudd in 2007.

At both ends of the spectrum, voters expect basically the same thing: more government intervention. In recession, they trust Labor over the Coalition to defend the social safety net. In boom time, they trust Labor over the Coalition to invest the proceeds of prosperity in social services and infrastructure. The twenty-first century has added climate change, water security and broadband to the traditional public-policy concerns of health, education and transport. This has reinforced the centre-left mood for the time being because these new challenges assume an active role for government.

As the lawyer said in *The Castle,* it is also about the vibe. Boom-time Australia is less greedy and less confrontational than it is in the acquisition phase that follows a recession. Even television programming has become warmer and fuzzier in recent years. Today viewers prefer the everybody-wins group hug of *MasterChef* or *Spicks and Specks* to the back-stabbing and grasping of *Big Brother* or *Who Wants To Be a Millionaire.*

The centre-left passed the right in the second half of 2005, according to Newspoll, as the WorkChoices legislation was being rushed through parliament and the China-led resources boom first began showering the budget with windfall revenues. Yet in retrospect the Ruddslide of 2007 was less significant than it seemed for Labor because even then it was being driven by the Greens. Labor won 52.7 per cent of the vote after preferences, but its primary vote was the lowest for an incoming government in the post-war era. At 43.4 per cent, it was around 6 per cent less than when it seized power in 1983 and 1972.

Plot Labor's primary vote over the past 100 years and two periods fall off the graph: the horror of the 1930s when the Scullin government was smashed after one term, and the decline since 1990. Between 1940 and 1987, Labor recorded just one primary vote below 40 per cent, in 1977. In the eight elections between 1990 and 2010, five have been in the 30-something death zone.

The party is a perverse victim of the Hawke–Keating economic miracle. The proportion of blue-collar workers has declined over the past twenty-five years. Professionals have taken their place, and they are drifting to the Greens.

Labor has traditionally worried about its male right flank, because of the split with the Democratic Labor Party in the 1950s and '60s and the more recent assault from John Howard. To get the DLP voter back, Gough Whitlam had to break Labor's hard-left faction in Victoria. This didn't offend the party's base because it dragged Victoria closer to the centre-left, where the rest of Labor's constituency already was. To meet the Howard challenge, Labor tried to edge to the right on the issue of border protection. Fine in theory, because that's where the nation was in the early noughties. But it doesn't work so well in a centre-left phase because for every conservative voter Labor rescued from the clutches of the Coalition, it lost another on its left to the Greens. The added complication is the feminisation of the workforce, which has made Labor generally more popular with women than men. Ordinarily this would have broadened Labor's base through the acquisition of conservative working women. But Labor lost as many women to the Greens as it did men.

The 2010 election should have marked the formal confirmation of power for the centre-left, with Labor winning a second term in its own right and the Greens claiming the balance of power in the Senate. It took an idiosyncratic prime minister and an inexperienced government to turn its mandate to mud. No other first-term Labor government has done so little with so much goodwill behind it. Past Labor governments could be trusted to hit the ground reforming in their first term. John Curtin recast the federation at home by claiming the income-taxing powers from the states. Gough Whitlam opened the door to relations with China. Bob Hawke floated the dollar. Even the successors to Curtin and Hawke made history in their first terms. Ben Chifley introduced the post-war immigration program and started the Snowy Mountains Scheme. Paul Keating delivered universal superannuation.

It is impossible to imagine modern Australia without these reforms. So what happened to the party of progress such that its return to power in 2007 found it unready and unable to lead?

The Rudd enigma explains some of it. He came to office with more than 600 promises to implement and a determination to win every day in the media. Ambition and indecisiveness linked arms to create an unusual model of leadership. Rudd talked, and talked. In the end, he was all door-stop and no delivery.

But Rudd was also the symbol of an era in which politicians viewed the electorate through the wrong end of the telescope. He wanted to be judged by his numbers, so he sweated the small stuff of the 24-hour news cycle and the fortnightly Newspoll. He tried to deal with the fragmentation of post-tariff Australia with a persona for every demographic. There was Kevin the erudite for the ABC set. Kevin the dag for FM radio and the Twitterverse. Kevin the genial dad for the Seven Network's *Sunrise* program. Kevin the bloke for *Today Tonight* and *A Current Affair.*

This wasn't an exercise in leadership but a form of politics as celebrity. The dignity of the office of prime minister has been reduced in stages since the 1980s. Hawke was the first rock-star prime minister, Howard the first common man to use talkback radio. Rudd wanted to be Hawke and Howard, so no medium was too trivial and no question too small for him to answer. An excess of accessibility diminished him so that voters could no longer discern between a major statement and a stage-managed appearance.

The responsibility must rest with the Labor caucus for giving Rudd the idea that government was just about him. Labor was dangerously short of institutional memory after eleven years in opposition, and it was happy to defer to the outsider who had finally beaten Howard for them. Only two ministers had previous experience in government: Simon Crean and John Faulkner. Crean says the Rudd model for governing didn't suit Labor because it placed too much emphasis on central control. The big decisions were taken by the so-called gang of four, namely Rudd, Gillard, treasurer Wayne Swan and finance minister Lindsay Tanner. When the kitchen cabinet met, ministers would be joined by advisers and bureaucrats.

"Narrowness in terms of cabinet processes can never work, particularly for Labor governments," Crean says. A reform-minded government shouldn't be afraid of internal debate:

> The concept of a smaller group for hard strategic decisions, I don't disagree with. But you've got to get the right mix between making the final decision and the consultative process that leads you to it.
>
> I think also there was a tendency to use and justify the strategic priorities and budget committee of cabinet [the gang of four] because of the threat of leaks, but my very strong view in all the cabinets I've sat through, seldom was there a leak out of cabinet. Now I'm not saying it didn't happen. But I think the more you understand the sanctity of the cabinet room and appreciate it for that, that's your best sanction against leaking, or idle tongues. And the great irony is the leak that almost rocked Kevin, the Godwin Grech leak, was [due to] the surplus of bureaucrats in the room. We were not operating as a cabinet, but a technocracy on many occasions.

Rudd inherited a command and control structure from Howard. In Howard's final year, the Department of Prime Minister and Cabinet "provided about 7500 detailed documents or briefings for the PM," Howard's former press secretary David Luff revealed. "Twenty a day. Every day. John Howard is to blame. Centralisation expanded under his watch. To cope with his hands-on approach, PM&C evolved to give competing, complementary advice, independent of others."

All that information, and still Howard lost office at the top of a boom, while Rudd couldn't hold it together for one term and his party lost its majority and almost surrendered government after it replaced him.

What is going on here? One explanation is that Rudd misread his majority, and with it the nation. Rudd was, essentially, a leader out of step with the public, a conservative with a centre-left majority. Rudd thought the nation was where he was, serious but cautious. But they wanted substance, and a little fun. Rudd didn't go to war for his side, as Keating, Hawke and Whitlam had before him. He hoarded political capital when the polls were strong, so that he had nothing to show his supporters, the people who brought him to office, when his approval rating collapsed.

Another explanation is that neither Howard nor Rudd could tame the media in the digital age. They confused presence with persuasion. They assumed that people were listening when the polls were in their favour. When a difficult issue arose, they tried to contain it by changing the topic. A cynical, though understandable, judgment was made about the electorate's attention span. The less the people thought, the better for the incumbent. Or so the theory went. But this method of feigned dialogue denied government a genuine connection with the community. Compounding the error was the desire to "win" each day's media – that is, to dominate the reporting. By definition, Rudd and Howard couldn't reshape public opinion to promote reform because they weren't prepared to tolerate a strong opposing voice as part of the process.

But neither of these explanations is sufficient. We are dealing with a system-wide crisis. Labor was unable to fulfil its first-term promise to be an agent of change because it, and the nation it served, had already lost the institutional means of reform.

The ETS and the mining tax and the back-sliding on immigration reflect the policy cowardice of the times. I will use these case studies to show why the reform model is broken, and that the Hawke and Keating governments, and the Howard government until 2000, knew a better way to run the nation. Consider what follows a medical examination of an ailing body politic. Let's start with the stethoscope: the media.

We Need to Talk About Kevin

Kevin Rudd never lacked substance as prime minister. His critics who called him a phoney, most notably Tony Abbott, mistook absence of policy achievement for absence of vision. Rudd had belief, and a prodigious capacity for soaking up a policy brief. What he lacked was the patience to stick with a debate long enough to assure public support for his position. The global financial crisis was the exception that proved the rule. It was the only challenge big enough to contain his intellect and draw out his greatest strength in a genuine crisis, the ability to ask one more question of his advisers.

Early in his term, I dubbed him our first federal premier. My piece ran on the day of the 2020 Summit in April 2008, when the prime minister was just about at the peak of his popularity. It was prompted by Rudd's disconcerting habit of dashing from issue to issue. I explained all this to him over a cup of tea in Melbourne four days after publication.

He didn't tick me off, although I had been warned that he was upset. But he did tick off a long list of things the government was working on. Without realising it, he confirmed the suspicion that he had taken on so many projects that he might end up getting nothing done.

Rudd feared that if a leader didn't feed the media, it would eat the leader. His colleagues confessed on coming to government that they felt as if they were in competition with Britney Spears. The assumption was that if government ministers didn't turn up, their Opposition counterparts would. The danger of saying no to the media even once was that they would not be asked back.

Like every leader I've watched closely, Rudd was a media junkie. John Howard says he would have been a journalist if he didn't practise law before entering politics in 1974. Paul Keating still keeps a clippings file of articles that interest or annoy, and is a regular newspaper columnist and letter writer. Bob Hawke and Mark Latham both tried their hand as *60 Minutes* reporters after they had left parliament. Tony Abbott and Malcolm Turnbull started out writing for the *Bulletin.*

Where Rudd parted company with his Labor predecessors was in having a severe case of journo brain – the condition that resets an adult's attention span to that of a five-year-old. This is not meant as a personal criticism, but rather a comment on a style of politics where winning that day's media overwhelms the business of government.

As with his centralised approach to governing, Rudd's media strategy was an extension of the previous regime's practice. The PM's press office operated like a mini publishing house. There were three press secretaries to put out the line and soak up the questions, and a battery of typists to pump out the transcripts of Rudd's every appearance. The bureaucracy was asked on almost a daily basis to produce what Rudd's people called "announceables" – some new piece of information or, if they were lucky, policy, which the prime minister could take with him to impress his media inquisitors.

Howard had developed the idea of an announcement a day to keep Keating off his tail in 1996. Howard's then chief of staff, Grahame Morris, explained the theory on the eve of that election. Policies had been held back deliberately so that the Coalition would have something positive to run with during the campaign. What are you guys going to cover, he asked: Keating attacks Howard, or Howard's latest announcement?

As prime minister, Tony Blair had a simple way to measure the demands of the 24-hour news cycle. He needed three issues a day to get him through his final election campaign:

> When I fought the 1997 election, we took an issue a day. In 2005, we had to have one for the morning, another for the afternoon and by the evening the agenda had already moved on. You have to respond to stories also in real time. Frequently the problem is as much assembling the facts as giving them. Make a mistake and you

> quickly transfer from drama into crisis. In the 1960s the government would sometimes, on a serious issue, have a cabinet lasting two days. It would be laughable to think you could do that now without the heavens falling in before lunch on the first day.

What worked in a campaign quickly becomes an organising principle for a new government. Rudd made not one but three announcements in the week leading up to the 2020 Summit. He appointed the first female governor-general, introduced a price-monitoring scheme for petrol, and proposed to extend childcare. The first was symbolic, the other two were ideas that had already been trialled at a state level.

Rudd appeared to be made for the digital age. He was an all-thumbs-blazing tweeter-in-chief with 800,000-plus followers. So long as his approval rating remained at Christ-like levels, the strategy seemed to be paying off. Senior Coalition figures confessed they were exhausted by the effort required to keep up with Rudd. But nothing he said stuck, apart from the odd, off-key quote such as "fair shake of the sauce bottle" or "political shitstorm."

Still, one can't blame Rudd for immersing himself in new media. Leaders have always looked for ways to cut out the press gallery and go direct to the voter, because they don't trust journalists to report their message faithfully. The digital age allows government and Opposition to become media organisations in their own right. They can direct their supporters to their home page, send them text messages, and encourage those who want to serve the cause to spread the word across the blogosphere. They are easy to spot. My niche economics and politics blog, *Meganomics,* is routinely bombarded with emails that begin with a patronising phrase along the lines of "I am a great admirer of your work, but you have got this one wrong." On one occasion during the 2007 election, I rang a contact and asked if he was behind that day's spike in traffic. Yep, he laughed. He had sent out a note to campaign workers at 11a.m. that morning telling them to "jam" my blog.

Yet political parties can never hope to dominate cyberspace because technology has lowered the barrier to entry for lobby groups, granting them the same access to voters. GetUp! niggles Labor, the climate-change sceptics annoy the Coalition. The latter used email to mount a successful challenge to Malcolm Turnbull's leadership of the Liberal Party in late 2009; the emails created the impression of a mass movement. But come election day, the Climate Sceptics party didn't even cross the legal limit of credibility. They garnered just 0.03 per cent at the ballot box, with fewer than 5000 primary votes across the nation, which was less than half the number achieved by the Socialist Equality Party. But almost 5000 messages in a politician's inbox can seem like a lot of angry constituents.

The institution of the media is almost impossible to manage today because it no longer respects politics. This is not an active choice on the part of journalists but a consequence of the information revolution. Each new-media entrant affects the way the old media go about their work. When the 6p.m. television news bulletins knocked off afternoon newspapers in the 1980s, the morning newspapers became more colourful. When talkback asserted itself in the 1990s, print journalists began to type as if they were shouting, and TV current affairs went from topical to trashy. The internet has made print even more aggressive and self-conscious, while forcing TV news into the credibility shredder of continuous broadcasting.

Old media have lost their financial power because advertising can no longer pay for large newsrooms. The evil genius of the internet is its ability to spook editors into cutting staff, while expecting more from those who remain. The demand for another story, another column, another bulletin, another live cross, routinely pushes the journalist into the gibberish zone. Too much information to process, too much to produce on any given day. What chance a considered policy debate?

Don't misread this as a cry for a slower, more liquid work day, when a long lunch could be rationalised as contact work. The internet has improved journalism in many ways. The problem is the black hole that comes with it. More news can't fill it because there are fewer reporters on the case. So we make up the difference with commentary. There is no right or wrong mix between news, analysis and opinion, but a form of medium creep is underway that turns journalist into player.

An article in the morning paper will prompt a couple of radio stations to call for a chat. Then Sky, then perhaps the *7.30 Report* or *Lateline.* Add another hour on the *Insiders* couch on Sunday, and it is conceivable that commentators will find themselves reheating the one insight across half a dozen forums. It becomes a form of politicking. A reporter goes on a virtual tour, like an author flogging their book. It is mostly harmless, until you count the hours that instant punditry takes away from the day job – time that used to be spent nagging sources, listening to debates and reading documents.

In this, journalists and politicians have converged in an alarming way: both the late Howard and Rudd governments spent far too much of their time feeding the beast. The result is a government that disappears up its own media mentions. In Rudd's case the problem began with him, but it also reflected the era. The pressure to be everywhere removed the sense of occasion when the prime minister spoke. There was no grand narrative to connect the individual announcements, only bewildering changes of agenda that left voters confused. One moment he was blokeing it up on a construction site, the next he was hopping on a plane to play diplomat at the United Nations.

Rudd didn't really know what he wanted to do with power. But even if he had had a plan, he would have found the media an unwilling conduit. To get his message to stick, he had to repeat himself. Neither Rudd nor the journalists had the patience for this traditional form of leadership.

I've witnessed three distinct phases in the relationship between politicians and the press. The 1980s was the incumbent's decade, when a federal Labor government convinced the press gallery that the Opposition was the better story. Labor used media monitoring to highlight rhetorical variations between Opposition spokespeople, and to play up the leadership rivalry between Andrew Peacock and John Howard.

We self-corrected in the 1990s by going on a form of government deathwatch, waiting first for the Hawke, then the Keating and finally the Howard governments to fall. In each case, our place in the pecking order was clear. They governed, we reported.

The past decade has diminished the influence of both leader and reporter. No one media group is dominant because the market is fragmented, but the media as an institution is more powerful than it should be because the never-ending news cycle has imposed a level of distraction on government that hobbles its ability to raise issues with the electorate. There is no tolerance for a long argument anymore because the public has been taught that every new day carries the promise of a blizzard of unique content.

The greatest threat the digital era poses to good government is not all those words, but the numbers. The desire for instant analysis leads politicians and journalists to the false comfort of the polls. There is a collective loss of confidence at work here. No one is really sure what voters will say to a new idea, so government and media ask them first through focus groups. It is no way to run a national conversation. Reform, by definition, must be preceded by a sustained debate. Rudd, and Howard before him, found that any issue that took more than a week or two to explain wasn't worth pursuing because they felt they couldn't afford the battering in the polls that this would entail.

Vox Populi

Polling has been a necessary evil in politics for decades. The first poll of Australian attitudes was published in the old Melbourne *Herald* in October 1941, and no party has ever had the will to honour its findings. It showed 59 per cent of people favoured equal pay for women, 33 per cent were against, and 8 per cent were undecided.

The first major-party leader to be paranoid about the polls, and the media organisation that published them, was Robert Menzies. His antagonist was the Herald and Weekly Times's managing director and chairman, Keith Murdoch. In August 1947, the *Herald* advised its readers that Menzies was a drag on the conservative vote. "If a federal election had been held in July, with someone other than Mr Menzies as leader of the Liberal Party, it is possible that a Liberal/Country Party Government would have been returned to power," the first paragraph of the article read.

Menzies and Murdoch engaged in an angry exchange of letters that make the modern rumble between Labor and News Limited resemble a contrived bout of WWF wrestling. In one letter, Menzies asked Murdoch: "Can you really believe that you can strike down the leader of a Party – when you do not suggest any alternate leader in the Parliamentary rank – and do no injury to the Party?"

Still smarting a year later, and not yet in government, Menzies wrote a prescient column for the *New York Times* in which he said that leaders were "anxious" about the effects of polling "on the practice of politics":

> If it serves to tell the politician of widely entertained errors which he must attack, well and good. But if it merely tells him to beware, because opinion is against him, many good ideas will, I fear, be abandoned.

The early polls also showed voters were wary of the non-English immigrants that were coming from Europe. My favourite was taken in 1951, the year after my father migrated to Australia. The Gallup poll asked voters "whether or not Australia should get immigrants" from a list of seven countries.

The Netherlands (80.6 per cent), Sweden (76.8 per cent) and France (59.4 per cent) recorded strong yes votes. So my News Limited colleague Andrew Bolt, the offspring of Dutch immigrants, was meant to be.

But not me. At the other end of the scale, we said no to people from Greece (only 42.7 per cent of Australians wanted them, which was lower than the yes vote for Malcolm Turnbull's republic). At least my mother country was close; Yugoslavia (33.5 per cent) and Italy (27.3 per cent) barely rated at all. The reason for the discrepancy can be seen in the response to Germany. Unlike the Greeks, who were our allies in World War II, the Germans had the advantage of "white" skin. The German approval rating was 55.4 per cent.

My mother came here in 1962. She might have had to choose America if the Menzies government had taken that anti-olive poll literally. But the more significant sliding door involves Arthur Sinodinos, Howard's long-time chief of staff. His mother, like mine, came to Australia after that poll was ignored. Without Arthur's advice, John Howard might well have been a oncer.

Immigration, like deregulation, was only accepted after many years of trial, error, adaptation and reconfiguration. We can score the 1940s and '50s, and the 1980s and '90s, as glory days for public policy because community prejudices and vested interests were confronted. While Menzies did not have much time for polls in his day, handled carefully they can assist the cause of reform. Bob Hawke and Paul Keating used polling to target marginal seats and to sharpen their arguments, but they never deferred to their pollster. The advisers they looked up to were the policy wonks.

"I would have been laughed out of court if I tried to overturn policy," says Rod Cameron, Labor's federal pollster from 1974 to 1990. "Could you imagine my going to Keating and saying, 'Look, the very thing you stand for, I'm sorry it's not testing all that well, you've got to drop it'? You would have had white-boards thrown at you if you asked him to overturn the float of the dollar."

The Hawke and Keating governments did face almost unbearable pressure from Labor's blue-collar base to slow the reform process. Ahead of the 1990 election, as interest rates peaked at 17 per cent, Bob Hawke toyed with the idea of a mortgage-relief scheme. There is no question that it would have been popular, but would the government have received any credit for it? Paul Keating told Hawke that voters would see the money as an admission that Labor had hurt them and that it no longer had faith in its own policies. Hawke dropped the idea, and won the election.

After Keating took the Labor leadership, the ACTU and most of his caucus wanted a tariff freeze. Again Keating would have none of it, although he did make a faux concession to protection by saying that his tariff cuts weren't as extreme as John Hewson's.

Labor likes to blame John Howard for allowing the polls to infect the governing bloodstream, but Kim Beazley was a willing adapter in the 1990s. The then Opposition leader was happy to let the polls do his thinking for him because for most of Howard's first two terms they showed Labor in front. Beazley was right about the unpopularity of the Howard government, but he misread its symptom – the rise of Pauline Hanson's One Nation protest party – as

Labor's cue to disown the reform cause. The Hansonites were seeking something neither side could deliver: the restoration of protection, the reduction of the Asian immigration intake and the removal of assistance to indigenous Australians. Beazley tried to appease these voters with an anti-GST crusade. The strategy almost worked until Howard shook his fist at boat people in 2001, which was the emotional play that returned the Hansonites to the Coalition.

The critical test of leadership, always, is whether the national interest is compromised in the search for voters. I believe Howard damaged Australia by using asylum seekers as political pawns. But he didn't extend the meanness of spirit to the regular immigration program. On the contrary, Howard became a big Australia prime minister. Immigration is the defining issue in the battle of wills between politicians and the polls, because voters, if given the chance, will always prefer fewer new arrivals. The temptation to follow the electorate was resisted by both sides of politics for sixty-five years, so what transpired in 2010 demands careful scrutiny. Howard can argue with some justification that he never allowed the argument about border protection to pollute the regular immigration program. The same cannot be said of Julia Gillard or Tony Abbott.

Howard, of course, wasn't always for a big Australia. In 1988 he suggested that Asian immigration be slowed in the interests of social cohesion. But the Labor government he faced back then knew what it stood for. Bob Hawke snarled every time the Coalition looked like breaking the bipartisan agreement on immigration. He met the argument, called out the intolerance, and split his opponents. Howard paid for his anti-Asian comments with his job in 1989. Andrew Peacock suffered in the 1990 election campaign for trying to sneak race back onto the agenda by opposing the so-called multi-function polis.

Paul Keating, likewise, stood his ground on reconciliation, and the moral investment he made through the Redfern speech, and then the Mabo native-title legislation, paid out handsomely for Kevin Rudd a decade later when he made the apology to the Stolen Generations. Simon Crean, and before him Arthur Calwell, would make the same point about opposing the wars in Iraq and Vietnam. There will always be times when Labor has to take a short-term hit in the polls to reaffirm its values. Otherwise its base drifts to a none-of-the-above party such as the Greens.

"It is not as if asylum seekers just became an issue," Rod Cameron says. "I had an issue of exactly the same dimension when Joh [Bjelke-Petersen] was running for PM [in 1987]. He was running around the country saying the Japs were taking the show over, and I said to people I reported to, 'This is a big problem. Here's a way if you present the argument this way, people might say, oh, there are two sides to this.' My advice was never to ignore the problem, but to face up to it."

Howard realised that he mucked up on Asian immigration in the late 1980s, but he took his time converting to the cause. A sluggish economy was his excuse to cut the intake in his first term, and the declaration of war on boat people at the end of his second term appeared to seal his reputation as a small-Australia prime minister. Then he changed, remarkably, and switched the colour of the immigration program from olive to yellow and brown. The numbers Howard decided to bring here in his final two terms made many on his own side wince, but it was the correct call. Australia had the world's fastest population growth rate when the global financial crisis hit in 2008. Take Howard's immigrants out of the equation and a recession would have been more likely. One of the things that set our economy apart from those of the United States and the United Kingdom was the behaviour of the property market. While their house prices collapsed – creating a vicious cycle of mortgage stress, reduced spending and job losses – large-scale immigration kept our house prices rising because supply was lagging demand. Ordinarily shortages would be read as a case of market failure, and they are. But they also played a valuable role in maintaining the confidence of Australian households to keep consuming while the rest of the developed world turned turtle.

The polls told Gillard and Abbott that voters had forgotten about the global financial crisis. They were more worried about congestion, about asylum seekers, about any darn thing really. Only a true leader would take these complaints to their logical conclusion and propose that Australia should shrink. And this is the point where the 2010 election troubled me. The first week of the campaign found both sides agreeing to something which no previous main party leader had suggested, and which no serious policy adviser would put their name to: reducing immigration when the economy is booming.

As one of the regulars on my blog pointed out: "Another 'Ah ha' moment. Both Gillard and Abbott agree that they want to stop people like them coming to this country. Good idea!"

Gillard was born in Barry, Wales, in 1961 and migrated to Australia at the age of four. Baby Julia had problems with her lungs and their family doctor suggested the Gillards move to a warmer climate. "So we came to Australia," her mother, Moira, told the ABC's *Australian Story.*

Abbott was born in London in 1957. His parents returned to Australia in 1960. "[His] first memory is of the steam train that took them from London to Southampton, where they boarded the SS *Oronsay* for the six-week voyage to his new country," his biographer, Michael Duffy, wrote. That makes him a boat person like my father, who took the ship from Greece to Australia in 1950.

Howard laughs when asked to comment on Gillard's sustainable Australia:

> Sustainable was her word for saying, "I'm now embracing the Opposition's policy on asylum seekers." We had a policy, it was tough on asylum seekers, I accept that. It wasn't popular with some people, it was popular with a lot of other people. But one of the things it did facilitate was a sharp increase in support in the community for orthodox immigration.

Many on the Labor side were uncomfortable with Gillard's Sydney-led race to the bottom on immigration. I had a number of big names prepared to dump on their party in the event that Labor lost the election. Sadly for this essay, the discipline of the hung parliament has zipped their lips. But the more revealing critic is Howard. It may burn Labor people to know that he has the most coherent argument against their poll-driven contortions:

> I very strongly believe that most Australians support a reasonably big immigration program providing it is for the benefit of the country. Most people look back on the last thirty or forty years and say that's been one of the good things we have done. It's been one of the big things that this country has achieved and it has been by and large bipartisan. Chifley started it, and Menzies continued it.

Howard isn't surprised that Labor turned the other way. The former New South Wales premier Bob Carr has been "against a large immigration intake quite unrelated to prejudice – he just thinks the place is overloaded." But Howard thinks the attitudes of Carr and Gillard threaten the national interest:

> Sure, in any country you are going to have infrastructure problems and all of that, but it has been such a good thing for Australia I would hate to see us lapsing into, or embracing, an attitude that does damage to the country. I thought Julia Gillard's utterances didn't seem to be the product of any long-term thinking or philosophy or whatever. They just seemed to be opportunistic.

Ouch.

But the same observation could be made of Abbott. In fact, it was the Opposition leader who first decided to play politics with the intake even though he was a supporter of a big Australia. In January 2010, as debate raged over the bashing of Indian students in Victoria, Abbott gave a speech calling for tolerance:

> Since 1970, an Australia that's four times richer has more than coped with a population that's two times greater. My instinct is to extend to as many people as possible the freedom and benefits of life in Australia. A larger population will bring that about provided that it's also a more productive one.

Yet a couple of months later he changed his position when he saw an opportunity to wedge Labor. By the election campaign, he was promising to reduce the intake by the end of a first term of Coalition government, regardless of economic conditions. If the definition of political cowardice is to turn against one's own publicly stated values because of the polls, then Abbott's stance on immigration is no better than Rudd's was on climate change.

Stop the boats – and close the immigration desk at the airport. Howard never made the link between border protection and the regular immigration program. In this he was merely continuing the bipartisan tradition on immigration that began with Ben Chifley and Robert Menzies. And on border protection, his position was really not that much different from Labor's – Keating had introduced mandatory detention, Howard had introduced offshore processing. The argument by the 2010 election was where, not whether. Labor claimed to have the more humane policy because it wanted asylum seekers interned in East Timor, a signatory to the UN convention, rather than on Nauru.

Abbott broke the seal on the regular program by joining the dots from the boats to the immigration numbers to the population debate. Gillard had a choice. She could have drawn on the Hawke example and called Abbott out for playing with the national interest. But she reached, instead, for a dog whistle of her own, the notion of a sustainable Australia.

No self-respecting leader would believe that public opinion is sufficiently informed to set the immigration intake. The numbers rise and fall from year to year depending on demand for labour. To cut when employers can't find enough skilled workers is to dare the Reserve Bank to raise interest rates to place a lid on wages. To tell China and India, the main customer for our quarry and a major supplier of our immigrants, that Australia isn't interested in offering their best and brightest a home anymore is to invite a belly-laugh across the Pacific. The Americans may be down on their knees at the moment, but their national survival instinct compels them to continue increasing their population. If we don't want them, they'll have them.

I'm prepared to argue that Australia is better off putting the people ahead of the services, and taking the risk of straining the environment in the short term, because the demands that come with a large intake are more likely to force governments to provide those services, and look after the environment over the longer term. Slowing population growth reduces our national income. It also excuses state governments from building new schools and hospitals, and reforming their planning codes to increase and improve the housing stock. As an example, just look at what happened to New South Wales over the past decade, when its population growth, and gross state product, lagged behind the rest of the nation. Congestion wasn't eased – in fact, it became worse – because Labor downed tools.

We should be expanding the immigration program to mine the youth belts of the United States, the United Kingdom and continental Europe. The time to grab these people is while their economies are on the mat. Pay their airfares if need be! It would be no different from the transaction that brought the Gillards to Australia in the mid-1960s. Forty years from now, our first American-born prime minister might look back at her mother country and say she wouldn't be a Yank for quids.

The business case for immigration often gets more publicity than it deserves because it is couched in the cost-benefit language of economic rationalism: you should accept these people because they will pay well above the reserve for your house. The better argument is the one that Chifley and Menzies made together after World War II: that we need more people to secure Australia. The threat today is not invasion, but ageing. Australia is one of only a handful of First World societies that can stay relatively young by keeping its doors open. Immigration doesn't reverse ageing, but it does slow it.

Gillard and Abbott offered no evidence to support their argument to shrink Australia, only polls.

***

So when did polling gain the right of veto over policies such as immigration and climate change? Federal Labor acquired the disease from its New South Wales division, according to a number of sources. The carriers were the New South Wales senator Mark Arbib and his ally Karl Bitar, who became Labor national secretary after the 2007 election.

Simon Crean puts it more diplomatically. I asked him how many in the parliament today are interested in policy. "I would say it is still more about policy in the House of Representatives. [But] it has been about politics in the Senate for some considerable time."

The ad man who came up with the "Kevin07" label, Neil Lawrence, says Arbib and Bitar have taken research too far:

> It's clear, and there is probably a majority consensus, that the turning point for Kevin Rudd was him walking away from the ETS. Real pressure advice was brought to bear from the national secretariat – from Bitar and his parliamentary compatriot Arbib – on the basis of polling and focus-group work.

Lawrence says polling took on a talismanic power. What the disengaged said in focus groups became policy because Arbib and Bitar were often able to convince Rudd and others that this was the last word in a debate:

> I think there was increasing deference paid to the polls in the Rudd prime ministership, [as] witnessed by the reversal on one of the three issues that he won the election on, that he had spoken so strongly about in terms we were all familiar with. I think it is self-evident the power that these things have come to wield.

Done properly, focus-group research can still act as an early warning device, alerting governments to the issues they need to keep talking about if they want to turn public opinion their way. But governments must be sure of their own beliefs before they go polling; they can't look to the electorate for advice on what to stand for. To read the polls as a cheat-sheet on what not to say, as Rudd and Gillard did, was to confuse means with ends.

Rod Cameron says Labor simply hasn't moved with the times:

> They are still using the Cameron formula, which was repeat, repeat, repeat the message, and when you are sick of it, repeat it some more. The assumption was voters will only ever see it once because they only get their political information on the Channel Nine news. That was true twenty or thirty years ago, but now [it's not].
>
> The other idea was [to] feed back to them what they say in the focus groups. Now that really worked for a decade, but that doesn't work

> anymore. They are awake to spin, they are ahead of the game, and they get their political information from a plethora of sources. So there is a lot more political noise at the water cooler.

Technology has allowed political professionals to collect more information. The mistake they made was to assume all that extra data brings them closer to understanding what is in a voter's heart. I suspect the impulses to xenophobia and greed, the fear of outsiders and the desire for middle-class welfare, are over-amplified by polling techniques that ask people what they don't like and what they want. Voters can identify problems, but they expect leaders to solve them, or at least to explain why things are the way they are. The medium has overwhelmed all else. Polling dominates the thinking of government and the media in almost equal measure. The range of numbers, and the rapidity with which they are updated, undermines a leader even when he or she is in front because any result below their best can be taken as a rebuke.

The newspaper opinion polls – Newspoll, ACNielsen, Galaxy – have become the cheapest form of content for a political reporter. No need to pick up the phone, just pull out the latest table and type. How is the government travelling? Is Brendan Nelson the most unpopular Opposition leader in history? Gee, look at the undecideds on the mining tax – do they know something we don't?

We've been living with poll-sourced volatility for two decades now. Arguably the first Opposition leader to lose his job with the assistance of the published polls was John Howard in 1989. The *Bulletin* had famously called him "Mr 17 per cent" and asked why he bothered. Between 1989 and 1991, there were three Opposition leaders – Howard, Andrew Peacock and John Hewson – and two prime ministers – Bob Hawke and Paul Keating. Recession can explain part of the churn in this period. What followed, though, was a form of perpetual crisis that bore no relationship to the economic cycle.

I know I'm whistling in the wind, but wouldn't it be nice if Newspoll were to go back to one poll per month? The *Australian'* s survey of federal voting intentions went fortnightly in 1992 and Newspoll made its reputation in the following year's election by picking the late swing to Labor. Don't change what works, right? Unfortunately, two Newspolls per month throughout a term provide too much temptation for mischief. Every half-smart backbencher can pull together a spreadsheet to show why their boss should be rolled. Lobby groups just have to wait for a couple of bad polls before they put the squeeze on government.

It may be a coincidence, of course, but there has been a dizzying turnover of political leadership talent since Newspoll went fortnightly. The Liberals were the first Opposition to have three leaders in a term between 1993 and 1996. The man in the middle,

Alexander Downer, was the first major-party leader not to contest a federal election. On the Labor side, Simon Crean was pulled down at the end of 2003, before he could face the people in the following year. Labor also had three leaders between 2004 and 2007. But these were mere dress rehearsals for the chaos of the past three years, when a first-term government had two prime ministers and a first-term Opposition had three leaders. The trend is clearly accelerating.

The trigger shifts with the circumstances. It may be the two-party vote that drives the coup, or it may be the preferred prime minister rating. It doesn't matter which number is highlighted, because an incumbent under siege has no counter to the accumulated weight of Newspoll. Even a rogue poll – the one in twenty that is outside the margin of error – can play a part. Newspoll had one apparent rogue in each of the past two terms. Instead of being brushed off as too extreme to be taken seriously, the survey sent the incumbent into a panic. Howard got his in the middle of the APEC leaders' meeting in Sydney in September 2007. Labor's two-party vote had jumped 4 per cent to an inconceivable 59 per cent. Howard asked Downer, his foreign minister, to take soundings on whether he should stand down as prime minister. The next survey found the Labor vote back to where it had been before the blip, at 55 per cent. Howard was able to assure his colleagues that he had made up ground during the crisis.

Rudd's turn came in November 2009, when Newspoll slashed an unusually high Labor vote by 7 per cent to 52 per cent. He assumed the trigger was the increasing numbers of boat people that were making a dash for Australia's prosperous shores. I suspect Rudd had forewarning that a bad poll was coming, because on the night before it was published he did five radio interviews in an hour and then appeared on the ABC's *7.30 Report.* The next Newspoll had Labor's two-party vote back at 56 per cent. Nothing had happened in the real world, but in the hall of polling mirrors Rudd had telegraphed his insecurity.

Perhaps little harm is done if a leader wastes his or her time making too many media appearances. But it becomes a concern for public policy when the prime minister brings out the chequebook to influence a single survey. In mid-February 2010, Newspoll found the Coalition had edged ahead of Labor on the primary vote, but still trailed 52 per cent to 48 per cent after preferences. Rudd made nine announcements in a fortnight, from 17 February, the day after that poll came out, to 1 March, the day before the next one was to be published. From mental health to counter-terrorism, from new road funding to the wind-up of the insulation program, the nine announcements betrayed a loss of perspective. By this stage Rudd had rejected the advice to call an early double-dissolution election on climate change. If there is a moment in history when a leader allowed himself to be bluffed by an opinion poll when he was in front, this was it.

I checked to see when Newspoll assumed its omnipotence in political reporting and political decision-making. It was more recently than I had anticipated. In the three months before the calling of the 2001 election, the *Australian* published forty-six articles that mentioned Newspoll. Ahead of the 2004 election, it was fifty-two articles, so no discernible change. But it jumped to 167 in 2007, and in the final three months of Rudd's prime ministership it was 161. That's almost two stories a day on average. (My name is on a few of those, I confess.)

The *Australian* no longer just publishes a report of the fortnightly poll and an accompanying analysis. The results are cross-referenced in all sorts of stories. Every other media organisation covers Newspoll as well. The film writer Michael Bodey tells me it is the same with movies. Box-office takings have become a standard point of reference. The question is not "Is this film worth seeing?" or "How was it made?" but rather "Look what it made."

Newspoll has created a self-fulfilling cycle of anticipation, interpretation, rejection and impatience for the next instalment. Best not tell the political junkies, but the polling the media uses is less reliable now than it was in the 1990s. An election-shaping segment of the population, Generation Y, can't be surveyed because it only uses mobile phones. The internet has complicated the market further; any firm can do a quickie poll online, increasing the risk of dodgy data getting into the mainstream news media.

Rudd lived and died by the polls, just as Howard did before him. When they were up, these socially awkward men felt invincible. No one in the party room dared speak out against them. As for the public servants, well, they were on performance contracts, so they could read the polls just like anyone else.

But when the trend-line moved against these leaders, they were forced to make exaggerated gestures of contrition. Rudd appeared on the ABC's *Insiders* at the end of his announcement spree in February 2010 and addressed the polls as if they were the nation itself:

> We are taking a whacking in the polls now. I'm sure we'll take an even bigger whacking in the period ahead. And the bottom line is, I think we deserve it, both not just in terms of recent events, but more broadly.

The published polls are a security blanket for political journalists, just as the private ones are for the main parties. We have poll-driven columnists tut-tutting at poll-driven politicians. Polls create a false sense of precision in what is an imperfect science. Yet politics is a contact sport, between leader and community. Those who rely on polling forget that voters know they are being watched, and manipulated.

Leaders

The juvenile tone of the 2010 election campaign was set by the Labor Party feud that preceded it. Not the 23 June confrontation between Kevin Rudd and Julia Gillard that saw the latter take the former's job, but Bob Hawke versus Paul Keating. Like two old bulls who didn't know when to stop charging, they tore through Gillard's election preparations with a dramatic escalation of their twenty-year public spat. Neither man would have meant any disrespect, but they seemed to catch the zeitgeist by forgetting that Gillard was about to face the people as the nation's first female prime minister.

Keating had read a part of Hawke's new biography by his wife, Blanche d'Alpuget. He thought the extract belittled his own achievements as treasurer, and wrote an angry three-page letter, which was hand-delivered to Hawke's Sydney office and then published on the front page of the *Australian:*

> This letter is written now, not simply to express my disappointment but to let you know that enough is enough. That yours and Blanche's rewriting of history is not only unreasonable and unfair, more than that, it is grasping. It is as if, Narcissus-like, you cannot find enough praise to heap upon yourself.

Gillard wouldn't take sides: "They are two great Australians having a passionate discussion about their politics. And I have to say as someone with an intense interest in politics, I am enjoying it."

As soon as Hawke and Keating were done, other former leaders would hijack the campaign itself. Rudd was the passive-aggressive father at the wedding, sending death stares to the daughter as she gave her reception speech. He invited the media to his local campaign events, then said nothing. When the leaking commenced against Gillard, he continued to say nothing. It was only after the polls showed Labor headed for defeat that Rudd became a team player again. But even then his body language betrayed him: he wouldn't give his leader the courtesy of looking at her during their stage-managed strategy meeting to assure voters they were on the same side.

Mark Latham was the mad uncle at the wedding who hijacked the microphone to tell the guests that love sucked and they should all go home. He took to the campaign trail to confront Gillard in a stunt that reflected poorly on him and the Nine Network. It's a moot point whether either man would have tried to crowd out a fellow male leader.

If you pit the recent past, Rudd and Latham, against Hawke and Keating, the source of Labor's 21st-century crisis is obvious. Rudd and Latham flew solo as leaders. They shared the loner's intolerance of their workmates. No one in the caucus was as good as they were, so they felt they had to do everything for themselves. Latham's 2004 election tilt was the training run for Rudd's government of one. Once their respective stints as leader faltered, each found they had no one watching their back. Latham resigned and Rudd was torn down. Then they turned on their colleagues without regard for the party they served. Rudd denies he had anything to do with the leaks that sent Gillard's campaign into the ditch, but someone close to him felt strongly enough about his departure to risk destroying a first-term Labor government.

By contrast, Hawke and Keating were grown-ups and party loyalists in government. They kept a lid on their personal rivalry for three successful terms that remade Australia. The public sensed that they had fallen out, but still re-elected them in 1990, and gave Keating a term in his own right after he toppled Hawke in 1991. The argument between these two giants is about who deserves the greater credit for what economists and political scientists around the world agree is the Australian miracle.

It is pathetic, of course, because the partnership was more important than the contribution of either individual. Hawke held the nation together and Keating made sure the policies added up and explained it all with memorable phrases. You couldn't have one without the other. But there is substance behind the bitterness.

Hawke's star shines brighter today with the hindsight of Howard and Rudd's centralisation of power. Hawke was blessed with a talented cabinet. The economic hardheads, most notably Keating, Ralph Willis, John Dawkins and Peter Walsh, gave the government its spine. The spending ministers, including Brian Howe and Neal Blewett, delivered innovative policies that respected both sides of the budget. Gareth Evans excelled as foreign minister and Kim Beazley starred as defence minister. None of these Labor heroes would have tolerated a micromanaging prime minister any more than it would have occurred to Hawke to try to tell them what their line of the day would be when they fronted the media.

Ministers were given free rein over their portfolios. Keating only wore two big defeats in his eight years as treasurer. Hawke denied him a consumption tax in 1985, which was probably the right political call. And he denied him again on telecommunications reform in 1990, when Keating wanted the old Telecom split up and exposed to full competition. Hawke got that one wrong, and the consequences of his veto are still being felt two decades later as Labor tries to separate Telstra's network and retail arms through the back door of the national broadband network.

Where Hawke and Keating excelled was in the manner in which they debated issues. Discussion papers preceded the release of important announcements so that the public had time to chew over the detail of reform. Trade-offs were routine. New taxes on capital gains and fringe benefits were offset by cuts to the top personal tax rate and the removal of the double taxation of shares. Real wages were held down to improve the profitability of business in return for increases in the social wage, including free health through Medicare and universal superannuation. There was a shared sense of mission with the press gallery, which enjoyed the joust on serious topics.

Lobby groups did complain often, and the media did run interference. The assets test on the age pension pitted the Hawke government against the Herald and Weekly Times before Rupert Murdoch reclaimed his father's company. But Hawke and Keating persisted. The public backdowns, like Keating's defeats in cabinet, could be counted on one hand.

Hawke never felt the need to prove himself against his ministers, as Rudd and Latham did with their much less intimidating ministries and shadow ministries. Hawke encouraged his staff just as much as he did his ministers, and looked up to his economics adviser, Professor Ross Garnaut, who was a key backer of the float of the dollar. A generation later, Garnaut would write the report on climate change for Rudd. But the prime minister preferred the advice of his pollsters to that of Garnaut.

Here is the other rub for the present generation of politicians: Keating didn't move against Hawke when the polls were bad. Keating wrote in his 2010 letter that he carried Hawke for four years through an "emotional and intellectual malaise" between 1984 and 1988. Most of his colleagues disputed the time-frame, but not the essence of his point: that he defended Hawke, even when they didn't get along. Keating wrote:

> No other prime minister could have survived going missing for that long. But with my help, you were able to. Kevin Rudd had two months of bad polls and you were the first to say he should be replaced.

In the days before the polling tail wagged the policy dog, governments assumed unpopularity as a necessary burden of office. They would have a tough budget in year one, deal with the unexpected in the second year, then, provided there was no last-minute incompetence, devote the third year of a term to re-election.

The power of the Hawke–Keating model was that their reforms won them credit with the electorate. It was a testament to tough love. The public said they hated each measure, but no Labor government before or since has been able to win five consecutive elections. Hawke won the fourth with interest rates at 17 per cent. Keating claimed the fifth with unemployment at 11 per cent. The magic rubbed off on John Howard, who won a second term by selling a GST at a time when unemployment was at 8 per cent.

Hawke and Keating entered public life at the end of the long post-war boom. Hawke became ACTU president in 1970, the year after Keating was first elected to parliament. Like Howard, who arrived in 1974, they believed that the only way to rebuild a sense of national purpose was to expose the economy to competition.

By contrast, the three Liberal leaders since the fall of the Howard government are all members of what I will term "the prosperity generation" – political beneficiaries of Australia's longest boom. Tony Abbott entered parliament in a by-election in 1994. Brendan Nelson was part of the conservative landslide of 1996. Malcolm Turnbull arrived in 2004.

On the Labor side are Rudd and Gillard, who were part of the 1998 intake. Before them there was Latham, who joined the club at the same time as Abbott.

The character trait that links this group, and the times in which they serve, is impatience. Latham lasted thirteen months as Labor leader before quitting altogether. Nelson was ousted after nine months as Liberal leader. His pushy successor, Turnbull, had fifteen months before he was knifed by Abbott. Rudd couldn't manage a full term as Labor prime minister. Gillard ran the government for three weeks before rushing to the polls.

A few months, a year at best, then back in the dole queue. Not enough time to master the craft, but more than enough to demonstrate your unsuitability. It would be unfair to call any of them flaky, yet this sextet is representative of a bipartisan decline.

What intimidates them are the metrics of voting intentions and personal ratings, and an unforgiving electorate. The voters, who can be hypocritical at the best of times, refuse to give leaders the chance to learn from their mistakes: one blunder and they are gone.

The prosperity generation did observe the odd crisis, but the danger would pass before the next Newspoll came out. The Asian financial meltdown didn't affect us in 1997–98. The US-sourced tech wreck of 2000–01 didn't make it here either. And the big one, the global recession of 2008–09, exempted just one Western economy: ours. Each escape would remind the prosperity generation that the Australian model worked, so there was no urgency to update it. The esoteric challenges of the future could always wait until after another election victory had been secured.

Deregulation meant government had less to do. With nothing at stake, the prosperity generation exaggerated the trivial. Latham played the SNAG card by asking Howard why his government didn't support reading to children. Rudd promised to monitor petrol and grocery prices to prove he was a better economic manager than Howard. Nelson dared Rudd to cut fuel excise by five cents a litre. Turnbull accused Rudd of corruption because he accepted a second-hand ute from a Brisbane car dealer. Gillard and Abbott promised to crack down on young hoodlums carrying knives. The phoney crises blur after a while. You keep expecting one or other combatant to wink at the camera to let the voter know they are putting on a show. But they mean it, every day, because the world ends for them if they don't win that day's media.

There was one more problem. The prosperity generation of politicians was drawn from a narrower gene pool just as the nation was becoming more diverse. Eight years separated John Button's Quarterly Essay, *Beyond Belief,* in 2002, and Rodney Cavalier's book *Power Crisis,* published immediately after the 2010 election. Button, another of the ministerial stars of the Hawke and Keating governments, compared the backgrounds of the MPs who came to power in the Hawke government with those of the Beazley Opposition. The first Hawke ministry had "a pretty good social mix":

> [It included] former farmers, businessmen, academics, lawyers and union officials, as well as a former engine driver, a teacher, a retailer, a waterside worker and a shearer. The government that reformed and deregulated the economy was not made up of political mandarins.
>
> Yet look at what a cloistered profession the parliamentary Labor Party has become. After Kim Beazley's vigorous campaign in the 1998 election, Labor returned to parliament with a party of 96

> members of vastly changed occupational backgrounds. Although one medical practitioner, one public servant and one engineer remained, no farmers or tradesmen did. There were two academics, two teachers and nine lawyers, but the social complexion had changed. What had replaced a broad spectrum of backgrounds was a new class of political operator who had been filtered through the net of ALP machine politics. Out of the 96 members, 53 came from jobs in party or union offices. These members described themselves variously as "administrators," "officials" and "electoral officers." There were also 10 former members of state parliaments and nine described as political consultants, advisers and lobbyists.

Cavalier, a former New South Wales Labor minister in the 1980s, deals with the disintegration of the state government over the issue of electricity privatisation. But the condition he describes applies across the party:

> Inside one generation, the catchment for parliamentary preferment is increasingly restricted to those who work on the staff of a minister, in the ALP office or an affiliated union ... The political class has captured the Labor Party in parliament and the machine. Its knowledge of Labor history and respect for Labor's traditions is zero; sub-zero really, as contempt for branches and the old ways is a staple of conversation.

***

The dividing line between the reform and the digital eras is the goods and services tax (GST), the last significant piece of policy that was pursued in defiance of the opinion polls. History records this as a decisive win for Howard, but the lesson he drew from it was, "Never again." I place Howard with a foot in each camp. The early Howard continued the Hawke–Keating project; late Howard wrote the manual for trivial government.

The GST almost killed Howard because he couldn't adequately compensate pensioners and self-funded retirees. They were his base, the over-fifties, and they had signed his political death notice twice before, first in the run-up to the 1998 election, before the GST package was released, and then ahead of the 2001 election, as tax reform was being digested by the community. The sequence is worth recalling because it set the dominoes tumbling for the rest of the decade, from the war on boat people to the use of government as an automated teller machine to buy off aggrieved voters.

Howard had found himself in the same first-term hole that Rudd fell into, with the Coalition primary vote at 34 per cent at the end of June 1998. But it never occurred to Liberal MPs to swap leaders before the election, then only three months away.

"At the time I don't think the deputy [Peter Costello] was as popular as she [Gillard] is now, I think that's the difference," Arthur Sinodinos told me on the day Gillard replaced Rudd. Looking back on the Coalition's first-term blues, Sinodinos said the government held together despite the polls because there was a unity of purpose in the cabinet. "They knew that their best chance of getting back was to have something to fight for, and that's where tax reform and the GST came in."

Howard needed the tax package to show he had a plan for a second term. Without it, both sides agree, he would have been a oncer. The government prevailed despite the loss of nineteen seats to Labor and a swing of 4.6 per cent against it.

The 1998 election proved to be a false dawn for Labor and its first-term Opposition leader, Kim Beazley. Victory had very nearly been achieved with a simple message: stop the GST. Labor anticipated that the GST would be an impossible tax to implement without hurting voters, so it bet the next campaign on the same issue. No introspection or policy reappraisal was deemed necessary, other than to disown the excesses of the Keating government; Labor relied on the polling that told it the GST was rat poison. The Australian Democrats had campaigned for the GST, but with food exempted. But Howard wasn't interested in a half-baked GST while the Tasmanian independent senator Brian Harradine was still talking. In May 1999, however, Harradine declared he could not support the new tax. Howard was stunned. He thought about sending the issue straight back to the people through a double-dissolution election. Instead he swallowed his pride and opened negotiations with the Democrats.

The parallel with the emissions trading scheme is fascinating. Kevin Rudd refused to compromise with the Greens after the Coalition blocked the ETS legislation in December 2009. He too passed up the opportunity of a double-dissolution election.

Rudd would have recalled that Howard was a reluctant negotiator with the Democrats. He agreed to their demands on food, and had to whittle back the tax cuts for higher-income earners to pay for the exemption. It represented 80 per cent of the original package, but Howard reasoned it was better than no GST at all.

"It would have been seen as a massive loss for Howard, after having won the election on this thing by the skin of his teeth that he couldn't get the thing through," Sinodinos says. "I think it would have finished his leadership and would have allowed Peter Costello to come up."

I spoke to Howard after the 2010 election. He said he never thought of the GST dilemma in terms of his own job. But he did concede the point that backing down would have rebounded on him:

> I don't know that I sat down and thought through what the implications for my leadership were. I

> just knew it would be very bad for the government if we had walked away from the GST, and something that is bad for the government is always bad for the boss.

The GST suffered teething problems in late 2000 and early 2001, which set off a chain reaction in the polls. The Coalition lost state elections in Queensland and Western Australia, and the federal seat of Ryan in Brisbane's leafy west in a by-election. On paper, Howard was in worse shape than he had been in 1998. He responded by sending the budget into deficit for one year to buy off the defectors. But only after saying he wouldn't compromise.

"I cease to be of any value to the Australian people if I do things that I don't believe in because of political pressure, and the Australian people will not respect me for that," Howard declared, a fortnight before buckling to the motor lobby. That handout, which abolished automatic indexation of the fuel excise, marked the formal end of the reform era. The motor lobby had only asked for a one-off 1.5-cents-a-litre reduction as compensation for the GST. Howard gave them more because he fretted that Labor might gazump him. It was not the way Hawke and Keating had done things. But it was the way Malcolm Fraser had governed between 1975 and 1983. Hawke and Keating were the leaders out of the box, and the passage of time has only made their governments appear more bold.

The fuel excise hand-out plays tricks with the memory of those on the conservative side. Howard's advisers who opposed it say it worked to kill a political problem. Yet the gesture didn't help the government in the polls: two months after it was announced, the Coalition's primary vote was back at 35 per cent. Howard needed another round of hand-outs to older voters, which were announced in the May 2000 budget, to stabilise the conservative base.

The nation's coffers are $6 billion a year poorer today without indexation. Double that cost for the removal of food from the GST, and you get an idea why no debate about tax reform in the future can proceed without another go at strengthening the indirect tax base to take the weight off personal income tax.

The GST exhausted Howard. It was one of those double-edged arguments where the media claimed the high ground of righteousness at the expense of good policy. We goaded the prime minister into adopting the GST after the 1996 election, then gave him grief on the detail even though he had won a mandate for tax reform in 1998. He said there would be no losers, so we screamed "gotcha" each time he was a decimal point shy of the perfection he promised.

Who could blame Howard for taking the opportunity to recast his leadership in August 2001 when a stricken boat of mainly Afghani asylum seekers rescued at sea by the Norwegian vessel the *Tampa* refused to return to Indonesia? The confrontation occurred only days before the 11 September terrorist attacks on New York and Washington. Border protection and the war against al-Qaeda were fused in the public mind for long enough to make voters forget what they thought was bothering them at the kitchen table. Howard became father figure to the nation, and then later, when the mining boom came, he added generous uncle to his persona.

Labor went into a long period of self-flagellation after the *Tampa* election. Mention boat people and they would curse that scoundrel Howard for allowing the redneck minority of the population to decide the circumstances in which campaigns are fought. Mention the hand-out machine and they would explode. Howard had perfected a form of cashed-up and lowest-common-denominator governing that rattled Labor's faith in the nation it wanted to serve. The mob were intolerant and greedy, Labor people often told me.

Maybe they were in the early noughties. But what never made sense was Labor's refusal to mount a counter-argument. The risk-averse model of campaigning, as Julia Gillard termed it, crept into Labor thinking in two distinct phases. First, economic policy was played down after the 1996 election, then social policy after the 2001 election. Don't mention interest rates, don't mention immigration. This allowed Howard to steal Labor's policy clothes. He convinced people that he, not Hawke and Keating, had written the nation's greatest economic hits.

Howard did nothing more on the domestic front in his third term but write cheques. He delivered the biggest expansion in middle-class welfare outside of a recession, making future reforms more difficult because there is a larger group of voters who won't want to be worse off. Howard only got back on the reform horse in his fourth, and final, term when he had control of the Senate. The temptation to avoid a repeat of the GST experience proved too great and he rushed his WorkChoices legislation into law.

A sneaky reform, dropped on the public without consultation and in breach of his election commitment to leave things as they were, it invited another community backlash. When the polls showed workers were worried about their pay and conditions, Howard reached into the show bag for another distraction. He seemed to make more announcements in his final year than in the previous ten. A takeover of the Murray– Darling, tax cuts, the Northern Territory intervention, a takeover of a single hospital in Tasmania, more tax cuts. But he had used up his Houdini credits, and WorkChoices became the main reason why the Coalition was defeated at the top of the boom in 2007.

Labor assumed the Howard method should be its method. Because Howard had given up on reform, Labor did too. Because Howard aimed at the wallet every time he suffered a wobble in the polls, Labor did too. This is why the party that held the nation together in World War II and remade it in peacetime wasn't in any shape to be an agent of change when power finally came its way again in November 2007. Labor governed by the conservative populist manual when the nation wanted something else. It was cowed by Howard, and captured by the polls.

Burning Down the House

There is a marvellous quote about Australia from the mid-1980s that is no longer supposed to be true. Australia, the *Economist* magazine observed, "is one of the best managers of adversity the world has seen – and the worst manager of prosperity." It has been twenty years since Paul Keating declared, "This is a recession that Australia had to have." For fiscal trainspotters, the anniversary falls on 29 November 2010. What is there not to love about this country? We've had two decades without recession while the United States has had two of them in the past decade. But the noughties was our least active decade for public policy in more than a generation. No nation should be so lucky that it delays reform indefinitely without suffering any consequences.

The last time Australia appeared to decouple from the United States was at the end of the 1960s, when they had a recession and we didn't. By 1975, we had joined them in an economic and cultural decline.

Australians simply didn't get along in the 1970s. Capital conspired when Gough Whitlam was in office, and the trade unions went on strike when Malcolm Fraser replaced him. Tax cheating became commonplace as respect for institutions crumbled. We got our national kicks when Lillee and Thommo hurled bouncers at the Poms, just as they got their kicks during the Great Depression when Harold Larwood halved Don Bradman's batting average in the Bodyline series.

History may not repeat, because the mining boom will be sending more money our way, but we have already suffered for the go-slow on reform. A leading indicator of future living standards is productivity, and Australia's effort in the noughties was its weakest since the 1970s.

Of greater concern is the precedent set by the two issues that crippled the Rudd–Gillard government: climate change and the mining boom. The debates are connected because they are globalisation's ultimate test of our temperament. The quarry is making us richer than we dared dream. Yet our customers are adding to the burden of climate change: China, in particular, is both a large emitter and a wrecker of the international push for an emissions trading scheme. Do we wait for the world and enjoy the party in the meantime? Or do we go first on the understanding that prevarication would only give the Chinese another excuse to obstruct collective action?

It shouldn't be that hard to solve the riddle because we have been here before. Australia began cutting its tariffs first, before the rest of the world, in the 1980s. If we'd waited, we'd still be waiting and the global financial crisis would have had a bullet with our name on it. By going early, Australia became match fit for the trials of globalisation. The cost of cleaning up the nation's energy sources is intimidating, but it is the next necessary step on our journey to self-reliance.

Both sides of politics understand that action delayed will eventually mean higher costs for everyone. They don't need a poll to tell them that whoever is eventually forced to place a price on emissions will have done it on less than favourable terms for themselves, and the nation, because they mucked around in the noughties.

John Howard put off a decision on climate change until the polls left him no choice. Too late, because it was this issue, along with WorkChoices, that brought Labor to power. It seems so long ago now, but at the 2007 election both sides promised an emissions trading scheme. Kevin Rudd tried to one-up the Coalition by saying he'd start his within the next term; Howard was only offering to do it by 2012.

The ETS failed in the first instance because Rudd played hard on the politics, but was too soft on the policy. He didn't cut Opposition leader Malcolm Turnbull enough slack for him to get the Liberal Party over the line. True bipartisanship involves sharing the credit for legislation. It doesn't need to be a full-blown collaboration, but the Opposition does have to feel good about its decision to jump into bed with the enemy.

Rudd didn't sell the ETS beforehand because the polls assured him that the public was onside. Then, when the legislation was being negotiated, he wanted to be both good cop and bad cop, making nice behind closed doors while attacking Turnbull in public. He thought the polls were still strong enough in late 2009 to force the Opposition into signing up for his scheme. But he was nervous about offending households and industry, so he caved in on the compensation package before anyone thought to ask.

The ETS to which Rudd and Turnbull agreed took more money from the budget to appease voters than it raised in revenue from the permits to emit carbon pollution, and the start date was pushed back a year, to 1 July 2011. A revenue-negative introduction for a reform of this scale is not necessarily bad public policy, provided it doesn't lose sight of the ultimate goal of placing a price on emissions; it is the change in relative prices that drives the investment in cleaner energy. This deal, though, was harder to sell because of its soft start.

Rudd unconsciously plagiarised both the WorkChoices Howard and the GST Howard in the way he approached reform, with too little community consultation and too much cash. He misjudged the national mood by seeking a position between the Greens and the climate-change sceptics. It was the same thinking that sent Julia Gillard on her election-campaign search for the disengaged voter in the middle. The centre doesn't constitute a majority without the believers.

Turnbull couldn't hold the Opposition together because the issue split the conservatives between believers and sceptics. He was told that he could keep his job if he blocked the government legislation, an offer he refused on principle.

The intrigue betrayed a lack of seriousness on both sides. Most of the players didn't really know what they were talking about. Rudd often stumbled when asked to explain how an ETS would work, and he failed to grasp the strategic importance of sticking to his already modified reform timetable.

The Senate defeat in December 2009 triggered a frenzy of meetings. Mark Arbib advised Rudd to call an early election for February or March. He wasn't alone in holding this view; Julia Gillard, Wayne Swan and John Faulkner were also urging Rudd to move quickly because they felt the sooner Labor went to the people, the better its chances of victory.

Faulkner was the most adamant that the election be fought on climate change. Rudd chose to wait, which turned the premise of the next round of discussions on its head.

What was lost in the subsequent recriminations was the time bomb Rudd had placed under his own leadership by procrastinating. Without an early election, the window for implementing the ETS in the next term had suddenly closed, because business would not get the year's notice that it required between the legislation's passage and the 2011 start date. This created a further complication because the ETS was already written in red ink into the budget with the hand-outs exceeding the revenue; now it had to come out of the budget. Why Rudd didn't think this through at the start of the year, before events overwhelmed him, is anyone's guess.

Asked to comment on the criticism of his role, Arbib replies: "I have been and always will be a big supporter of a price on carbon – you can't reach the greenhouse reduction targets without it." He will not discuss his private conversations with Rudd.

People close to Rudd still don't know why he baulked when one poll said he would win an early election on the ETS, then folded when another said he might lose if he didn't drop the ETS.

The question that Gillard and Swan should address as his ultimate executioners is why they thought Labor could get away with abandoning its conviction on climate change. Even so, Rudd bears ultimate responsibility: this was a leader's call, and he picked the wrong poll to take at face value.

The pollster Tony Mitchelmore says leaders who take the electorate's complaints too literally sacrifice the very thing that allows them to shape public opinion: their authority. Mitchelmore stopped doing work for federal Labor soon after it went into government. When he returned to the field to conduct focus groups for his own business last year, he detected a growing disquiet about Rudd. It wasn't issue-specific; rather, it was his government's lack of clarity that made people wonder whether they really knew him.

"In September last year, he was still rating well, but in the groups they were struggling to describe him," Mitchelmore says.

> They weren't sure who he was. Some people who did have a definition of him, their picture was very different to when they elected him. Because there was that mismatch, they assumed it was just fraudulent behaviour, he was not being genuine, it was just an act.

The ETS reversal caught those doubts and amplified them. On this the pollsters and the policy wonks agree. Ross Garnaut used a lecture during the 2010 election campaign to savage the Labor Party that used to look up to his advice:

> The position on climate change is weak only because of an extraordinary failure of leadership. The failure is a product and represents the nadir of the early 21st-century political culture, in which short-term politics and accession to sectional pressures has held sway over leadership and analysis of the national interest. Those political advisers who turned out to have greatest influence over former prime minister Rudd weighed undoubtedly strong resistance from special-interest groups, and inchoate reactions from partially informed members of the community, above more

> fundamental determinants of political success. They played down the unusual reality of majority support for a measure involving major structural change in the economy. More fundamentally, they ignored the crucial respect for the role of leadership in the democratic process. In accepting their advice, Kevin Rudd abdicated the leadership of Australia, and set the scene for the destruction of his prime ministership.

The Liberals were no better; they too let the polls do their thinking for them. Tony Abbott took the Opposition leadership by one vote in December 2009. He didn't expect to win until the favoured candidate, Joe Hockey, was counted out first in a three-way ballot with Turnbull. Abbott had been a supporter of the ETS before he was against it. He said the science was "crap" but he still felt the undertow of the polls dragging him towards a gesture on climate change, so his first act as leader was to promise $3.2 billion in hand-outs over four years to buy emissions cuts.

He ran three fantastically contradictory lines. He agreed climate change was happening, while questioning the science. He said Rudd's scheme was a great big new tax on everything, even though it was revenue-negative. And he had his own budget-draining plan to buy reductions in carbon pollution from industry and farmers, while simultaneously arguing that only a Coalition government could pay back the debt and end the waste.

On releasing his "direct action" plan for climate change in February 2010, Abbott must have known the gods were smiling on him. In the reform era of the 1980s and '90s, any party that announced new spending without saying where the money was coming from would have been monstered by the media, the economics profession and business groups. Kim Beazley or Andrew Peacock would never have been allowed to get away with un-costed policies by the Howard, Keating or Hawke governments. But Abbott evaded even token scrutiny, because his climate-change gesture was a one-day wonder and it was judged to be no more than a piece of political theatre.

Treasury had sharp words for both sides in the briefs it prepared for whoever won the election. The blue book for the Coalition said, cuttingly, that using the budget, rather than a market mechanism, to tackle climate change is not in the national interest. Treasury reminded the Coalition that it was already committed to reducing emissions by 5 per cent below their 2000 levels by 2020:

> [This] cannot be achieved without a carbon price unless significant economic and budget impacts are to be imposed. A broad-based market mechanism which prices carbon, driving large scale abatement through long-term investment in low emissions technologies and changes in behaviour

> by both producers and consumers across the economy, is the only realistic way of achieving the deep cuts in emissions that are required. Market based mechanisms represent the lowest cost pathway when compared with regulation, mandatory standards or budget-financed initiatives ... Moreover, many direct action measures cannot be scaled up to achieve significant levels of abatement anyway, and for those that can be scaled up, the cost per tonne of abatement would rise rapidly, imposing further costs on taxpayers and consumers.

There is an understandable tone of frustration in the document: "Too much time has already been wasted – for which the Australian community will necessarily pay a higher price."

Defending the government's approach, Julia Gillard says that while it is easy to criticise with the benefit of hindsight, Labor nearly succeeded:

> We went for a political consensus, and we almost got there. [But] because the focus was on driving that political consensus, the complex conversation with the electorate was not being had and the absence of that complex conversation showed in the election.

That the Rudd model almost worked does not redeem it. The very fact that he relied on Turnbull, who was the most passionate advocate for action in either of the main parties, meant Rudd was seeking the path of least resistance by negotiating with a believer. The more serious conversation had to be had with the public.

Dealing with climate change became more difficult after the global financial crisis hit because business wanted a breather. Rudd and Turnbull were sympathetic and settled on a package which made the transition almost pain-free for business, but that gave the Greens the excuse to sit on the sidelines when the Abbott coup overturned the bipartisan agreement. The deference to capital is puzzling because it routinely lets down both sides of politics. The last notable example of a business-led reform debate was in 1997, when the Australian Chamber of Commerce and Industry and the Australian Council of Social Service gave the Howard government the political cover to revive the GST. This is how the business lobby used to operate under the Hawke and Keating governments. It would argue for deregulation on the grounds of self-interest, of course, but it was really doing the government's bidding. The Business Council of Australia would start a debate to the right of Labor, giving the government room to convince its own constituencies in caucus and the trade unions to take a seemingly more moderate position. If the electorate sniffed a set-up, it didn't mind because the image of a Labor government being helped along by business suggested the national interest was driving policy.

Rudd and Turnbull gave business what it asked for, and more – just as Howard had with the motor lobby over fuel excise. The pattern of appeasement has convinced business to revert to its pre-1980s state, when it behaved like an impatient child in the lolly shop, trying to force its open hand to the front of the counter.

So if the kids get too greedy, why not punish them by taking away their allowance? You could almost hear the impulse to retribution override Rudd's diplomatic brain. He'd been so accommodating to business on the ETS and yet it wouldn't go to war for him to convince the Coalition to hold its nerve. Then he deferred to those on his side who said, "Cut your losses on the ETS," and he was punished for doing so by the polls. Well, if the people want conviction, let's try tax reform.

All the political ills of the past decade – the policy indolence, the partisan self-obsession and the bloody-mindedness – found their most toxic expression in the mining-tax debate. The rule book for reform was torn up.

Like everything Rudd took on, it was a terrific idea at the time. At the 2020 Summit, tax reform was the suggestion that had most delegates nodding. The head of Treasury, Ken Henry, was given the task of conducting a root-and-branch review of the tax and payments systems when the budget was still in surplus. Only two items were off-limits: the rate and base of the GST, and tax-free superannuation payouts.

Henry's advice to the incoming Rudd government had been the same as it had been to the Howard government: the best way to return the surplus to the public was in the form of lower taxes. All other spending proposals were not as efficient in economic terms. Interestingly, the public didn't see it that way, telling the pollsters they preferred increased spending to tax cuts.

What no one appreciated in the first half of 2008 was that our surplus was a sign of something about to explode. The global financial crisis promptly sent the budget into record deficit, as the world economy reset our income clock. The government could have pushed back the Henry review until the budget could afford it, or narrowed its scope. But Rudd being Rudd, he insisted they continue as if nothing had happened.

Tax reform and a generous increase in the age pension added to an already over-full plate. Then Rudd became distracted by problems with the home-insulation program, negotiations with the states over health reform, an arm-wrestle with Gillard and Swan over the ETS, child care and preparations for the budget. Rudd sensed he had over-committed and folded under the pressure. His public demeanour suggested he was in need of a holiday. Privately, he lost focus and allowed the work to pile up. By February 2010 his colleagues were fed up, although it was still four months before he would lose the leadership. Gillard was the last to move against him because she assumed that he would snap out of his funk in time to get back to doing what he does best: campaigning. But he wasn't ready to call the election when Gillard and others were advising him to – by August or September – because the fight with the miners had taken on a life of its own.

The mining tax was another WorkChoices moment, a complex policy dumped on the public with no warning. The industry, despite protestations to the contrary, knew what was coming and supported the concept of a profits-based tax. What it objected to was Labor's timetable, which appeared to place decision before consultation.

The Henry review and the government's initial response were released in the week before the May 2010 budget. The prime minister and treasurer worried that their tax package would be seen as too timid, and that's how it was judged by political and economic commentators, myself included. There was no warning of a brawl in those early days because the two biggest miners, BHP and Rio, were muted in their first statements.

Henry had recommended a profits-based tax on mining to replace the production-based royalties levied by the states. The industry agreed with the theory, it just didn't like the way this tax was framed.

While the government embraced the review's mining-tax proposal, it had its own ideas about how to distribute the $18 billion a year in revenue. Henry wanted mining royalties abolished, but as Labor didn't want a fight with the states, it offered the miners a refund for the royalties they had already been charged, at a cost of about $8 billion a year. Henry wanted the mining tax to fund a five-cents-in-the-dollar reduction in the company-tax rate, which would account for the remaining $10 billion in revenue. Labor settled for a two-cent cut, or $4 billion for companies, and used the other $6 billion to pay for tax breaks for small business, bank interest income, infrastructure spending and to boost the superannuation levy from 9 per cent to 12 per cent of workers' wages. The Henry review's grand bargain to transfer the proceeds of the mining boom to the rest of the economy through a reduced company-tax rate had been diluted.

A few quick points on the detail. The complaint that the resource super profits tax (or the "Aretha Franklin tax", as it was dubbed by Treasury officers because the acronym RSPT reminded them of her version of Otis Redding's song "Respect") amounted to double taxation was nonsense. Mining has always been taxed twice. The argument that mining already paid its fair share was also wrong. The Minerals Council of Australia said its members faced an above-average corporate-tax burden. Not true. On the figures the council supplied, mining enjoyed the fourteenth-lowest effective company-tax rate out of nineteen sectors. It paid a lower rate than manufacturing and construction, the very sectors it was crowding out.

The miners have been making money because their main customer, China, has inflated the world price for our coal and iron ore. A mining tax on those windfall profits poses no credible threat to the kitchen table because the Chinese wear the cost.

But the cash they send us does mess with the real economy. The mining boom soaks up every available investment dollar, and while not a big employer in its own right, the wages the resources sector is prepared to pay give every other business nightmares because its staff might want the same. The crowding-out extends to governments, which are forced to compete with the miners for scarce labour to build roads, hospitals and schools. Royalties don't level the playing field. A profits-based tax doesn't either, but it does provide a more efficient mechanism to redistribute wealth to the rest of the economy.

The miners saw the Aretha Franklin tax as a form of nationalisation. In principle it gave taxpayers a 40 per cent stake in each mine. They collected 40 per cent of the profits above a normal rate of return, and covered 40 per cent of the losses. The miners said the guarantee on losses was worthless because no bank would lend them money on the strength of it. The government took time to concede this design flaw. It might have avoided this particular problem had it been willing to release the tax in draft form for discussion, and had the miners been prepared to engage in good-faith negotiations.

Where the government and the miners blundered together was in allowing the argument to escalate into an open advertising war. The miners were able to strong-arm the government because the prime minister had lost what his colleagues termed "the crutch of Newspoll." Even so, Rudd welcomed the brawl because he thought it would be the solution to his problem on the ETS. Show enough of his stubborn side to voters and they'd forget that he'd walked away from his principles on climate change only a month earlier. Yet Rudd's belated display of toughness came across as a prime-ministerial tantrum. Labor people were stunned when he resorted to xenophobia with the clunky observation that "these massively increased profits built on Australian resources are mostly, in fact, going overseas." They scratched their heads again when he broke his solemn promise not to use government advertising to run political campaigns.

Successful tax reforms of the past had been preceded by tax summits and discussion papers, as was the case with Paul Keating's changes in 1985. The GST package of 1998 was released after a year-long softening-up process in which the Coalition punched away at the old indirect tax system. The idea was to flush out opposition, address unintended consequences and provide the voters with sufficient information that the government had the public-relations edge over vested interests. The mining tax should have been in the public domain at least three to six months before the May budget, not one week before. That way the public focus at budget time would have been on the tax cuts associated with the reform.

Julia Gillard and Wayne Swan believe that Rudd could not have resolved this dispute before the election, and it was pivotal in their decision to move against his leadership. Rudd would disagree, but that is immaterial because he had done enough damage already in the way he conducted the tax debate.

None of this excuses what the mining industry did. To run interference against government legislation before it has been released sets an American precedent for our system, in which policy is dictated by those with the deepest pockets. The miners probably think they were just exercising their democratic right to call out a bad tax. But this was an election year, and the miners were seeking a veto no lobby is entitled to – to deny a government the right to set taxation rates. The miners wanted to destroy the tax in the court of public opinion before the government even had a chance to settle the detail in consultations with them. The place for lobbying is the parliament, where every citizen has the same theoretical right to influence the debate through their local member. If the parliament passes legislation the miners don't like, then all bets are off. Take it up with the voters at that point, as the ACTU did with its campaign against WorkChoices. Any intervention beforehand defies a basic principle of democracy, that power is vested in the people through their parliament.

The democratic theory is one thing, but there is also a pragmatic reason why governments should never allow global firms to dictate policy. Miners have the same power as financial institutions to bring down national economies if they borrow too much. At first blush, the global financial crisis is primarily a failure of regulation and oversight. Wall Street had convinced the US government and the US Federal Reserve that the interests of the firm and the nation were the same. Leave us alone to make our billions, and we'll all be better off. Australia avoided catastrophe, in part, because our banks were well behaved and very well regulated. They still carried the scars of the 1990–91 recession when two of the big four banks almost went broke.

The big mining companies say they kept us out of the 2008–09 global recession because they continued digging while the rest of the developed world crashed. The focus groups certainly agreed with this proposition. The research had told Rudd to stop talking about the global financial crisis because the punters didn't give him credit for the effect of his government's stimulus spending. So he left a rhetorical gap that the miners were happy to fill by saying that they, not Kevin, had stepped in when the nation needed help.

With friends like these, who needs government, right? One month into the mining-tax war, Rio's chief executive officer, Tom Albanese, went on Sydney talkback radio to assert his claim to be Australia's sugar daddy.

"I want to invest in Australia, I want to put billions of capital into Australia," Albanese told Alan Jones. With his host egging him on, Albanese came close to claiming he had personally saved us.

> ALBANESE: Australia benefited from the mining industry –
>
> JONES: Absolutely.
>
> ALBANESE: – to keep these –
>
> JONES: Absolutely.
>
> ALBANESE: – the whole economy out of recession. And that helped everyone.
>
> JONES: Yeah, I agree.
>
> ALBANESE: I'd been travelling all over the world last year, in the depth of the recession, and the only place anywhere in the world where people were actually in restaurants was in Australia as they were the only ones in the world that had any money.
>
> JONES: Good on you.

Indeed he was travelling the world in 2009. Rio was the company that almost brought the global financial crisis home to Australia when it got caught with a mountain of debt. Albanese sought to keep the banks at bay through a deal with the Chinese government. Now that was real sovereign risk, not the straw-man version the mining companies would erect in order to argue against the Aretha Franklin tax.

As the global financial crisis continues to unfold around the world, what troubles policy-makers is the prospect that a government will default on its debt. When governments default, they can either have their debts forgiven, or they can sell a bit of themselves to another nation. Rio was prepared to give Chinalco, a Chinese state-owned enterprise, the opportunity to lift its stake in the company to 18 per cent, at a fire-sale price of US$19.5 billion.

The conflict of interest was obvious to both sides of politics. Rio lobbied the Rudd government for approval. In fact, it begged, according to informed sources. Fortunately, the Chinese talked themselves out of the game by propping up the global economy. Their stimulus package put a floor under commodity prices and this allowed Rio to walk away from the deal in June 2009. The lesson of this transaction is this: beware any CEO who thinks their bottom line equals that of the nation.

In his book on the Chinese Communist Party, the journalist Richard McGregor makes a compelling case that Chinalco was not only state-owned, but state-influenced. For its part, the Chinese government insisted that the aluminum company and the party were at arm's length. McGregor writes:

> Not long after the deal collapsed, four of Rio's China-based executives were arrested in Shanghai by state security on allegations of bribery and commercial espionage. It was no wonder that political opponents of the deal in Australia were able to portray Chinalco as an agent of the state. For a Party on a mission to convince sceptics that Chinalco was an independent entity, it was another wrenching own goal.

The miners-saved-the-economy line overlooks one other important fact. Queensland, the most populous mining state, suffered the sharpest drop in state income during the global financial crisis. Queensland's gross state product grew by 0.3 per cent in 2008–09, well behind the national rate of 1.1 per cent. Only New South Wales went closer to recession, with growth of just 0.2 per cent. But New South Wales had been underperforming for a decade; this was the Sunshine State's first below-average effort in more than twenty years.

It is possible to sympathise with Rudd for wanting to poke the miners in the eye, but revenge doesn't serve the national interest either. The mining-tax debate caught all the bad habits of the past decade and packaged them into a reality TV show.

And then something funny happened on the way to the election. After Gillard replaced Rudd as prime minister, Labor's vote rebounded and the miners were suddenly keen to cut a deal, and the government was eager to give up on a few of its principles as well. Gone was the 40 per cent rate on super profits and the 40 per cent refund for losses. A 30 per cent minerals resource rent tax took its place, and it would apply to coal and iron ore only. It delivered almost as much revenue as Ken Henry's original elegant design, because the three big miners, BHP Billiton, Rio Tinto and Xstrata, had revised up their profit expectations. A lower rate on a larger pile of money seemed to satisfy both sides. But like Howard's GST deal with the Democrats, the rollback meant someone would lose a bit of their tax cut. The bunny was the non-mining business sector, which saw its company-tax cut halved by $2 billion, from two cents to one cent in the dollar. Labor would say "serves them right" for not sticking up for tax reform.

The lightning speed of the accommodation meant that the detail of the tax would have to be resolved after the election. Tony Abbott could have walked away from the fight at this stage, but he continued to oppose the tax. Like his position on climate change, it was a simple political calculation: Labor was on the nose in the mining states, so why let it off the hook even if the miners were happy?

When Rudd's polling honeymoon ended, there was no dialogue, just drama. That may have been the former prime minister's doing. Yet even Rudd's opponents in the government say the behaviour of the miners was shameless. In the non-mining business community, there was concern that the campaign had gone too far. The idea that any industry would seek to topple a government made some well-known business chiefs uncomfortable, according to a trusted conservative source. But they didn't speak out, and have no reason to do so now.

Wayne Swan says he was "disappointed by the distortions and the dishonesty encapsulated in that highly partisan but well-funded campaign":

> The truth is there was consultation, before and after the announcement, but that consultation was unfortunately coloured by big spenders like Mr Clive Palmer trying to drive a political outcome rather than a good economic outcome for the country. Australians would be far better served if arguments were won and lost on their merits and not on the basis of how much money people can afford to throw into an advertising campaign.

The treasurer says the Opposition played spoiler because it thought that would win it the election:

> They are very anti-reform now. If they can't support an NBN, which is a rolled-gold case in economic theory and microeconomic reform, or a simple profits-based tax, or a boost to super in

> a capital-hungry nation, they have gone completely native.

The miners and the Coalition were following the lead of the trade unions. Both had seen what the ACTU achieved in John Howard's final term when it ran a national advertising blitz and a marginal-seats campaign against WorkChoices. The Liberals' federal director, Brian Loughnane, said this had never happened before:

> For the first time in our history, a third external force has intervened in our political process with resources greater than either of the major political parties. I believe this is an extremely unhealthy development. If disclosure of campaign spending is to mean anything in this country, the ACTU should be required to publish a report setting out details of how the $30 million it allocated to the campaign was spent.

Ben Chifley would beg to differ, because the banks had campaigned against their nationalisation at the 1949 election. Loughnane also forgot to mention that the Howard government spent much more than $30 million on taxpayer-funded ads to promote WorkChoices, but his point was nonetheless valid. Political parties and governments shouldn't be forced into these sorts of bidding wars. My preference would be to ban all third-party political advertising. Vested interests can make their case to journalists, who can then use that information to scrutinise government policy.

The truth is that lobby groups with more members or cash than the main parties have always had the power to thwart governments. What has changed is that labour and now capital have had a taste of the drug that is the media and polling cycle. Government has never seemed weaker, and the opportunities to intimidate it will only increase with a hung parliament.

And yet ... in mid-September 2010, days before the first sitting of the hung parliament, BHP's chief executive officer, Marius Kloppers, called for a carbon tax, a policy Gillard had explicitly ruled out for Labor's second term. This was head-spinning stuff. The mining companies had helped to bring down one Labor prime minister. Now the biggest of them all, BHP, was trying to help the new Labor prime minister find her reform voice.

Optimists would say that business and the Gillard government have taken their first tentative step towards a reform partnership. But let's see what happens when Labor gets into trouble in the polls again, or if an early election is called.

The Green and the Grey

Pick a poll, any poll, in the two years when Kevin Rudd was surfing a wave of national goodwill, or in the first four weeks of Julia Gillard's prime ministership, and even the most one-eyed conservative would concede that voters were keen for Labor to succeed. To bugger it up not once but twice in the same term required a special form of political deafness on the government's behalf.

Rudd proved to be too conservative for the nation he led, while Gillard's campaign for re-election was too cynical. But the problem goes deeper than any individual's failure. Labor in office suffered a return of the identity crisis that had plagued it in its wilderness years in Opposition, when each federal defeat to John Howard would yield the same basic analysis: the party had given up its soul to the machine. In 2010 the electorate got it right by taking away Labor's majority, while at the same time leaving Gillard just enough wriggle room to secure minority government. The alternative, a return to Coalition rule after just one term in the sin bin, would have made little sense without an agenda. And let's be frank: Tony Abbott had no policies to speak of that addressed the challenges facing the nation. He thought climate change wasn't real enough to warrant action, and that the mining boom didn't pose a great enough threat to the rest of the economy to necessitate the introduction of a profits-based tax.

The task for the Gillard government is, in essence, the same task that the Rudd government could not handle when it was popular. Australia is prosperous and voters want the proceeds of the boom to be invested wisely on their behalf. The mining tax and putting a price on carbon pollution are more than just political symbols now for Labor. They will test whether the nation is capable of reform given the constraints of a hung parliament.

The 2010 election turned politics upside down by splitting the House of Representatives along state lines, while creating a historic Labor–Greens metropolitan majority in the Senate. It is not quite what the founding fathers had in mind, because the lower house was meant to be the people's chamber, while the interests of the states were to be protected in the upper house.

The result, in a nutshell, saw the mining states abandon Labor, while the southern states swung against the Coalition. New South Wales couldn't make up its mind between the main parties. Women backed Julia Gillard, men sided with Tony Abbott. The old went for the Coalition, and the young, well, this is where the game really changed. The Greens gained the support of 25 per cent of men aged 18–34 years, and almost 20 per cent of women of the same age.

Julia and Tony, meet Generation Y, the voters who threaten the major-party duopoly.

I had wondered for some years what would happen to Generation Y when it faced its first recession. Born in the 1980s, this group came of age in the Howard years with a social outlook that was the antithesis of the prime minister's. Their self-absorption suggested that they would become hysterical when the easy credit ran out. Instead, the global financial crisis found them in better shape than their baby-boomer parents and their big brothers and sisters in Generation X. They behaved as the deregulation manual said they should by agreeing to reduced hours to save their jobs. When the economy improved, they figured they could either return to full-time work or swap employers.

The stress was felt further up the age scale, by Generation X and especially by the baby boomers born in the 1950s. For people aged in their fifties who are at or near retirement, the Australian economy had long seemed like a beautiful dream. These baby boomers may have suffered in the recession "we had to have," but they got the best of the recovery that followed. If they played their property cards right, they would have bought in at the bottom of the market and seen their capital gains explode over the past decade. What could they possibly have to complain about when the global financial crisis hit? Plenty. The fifty-somethings had borrowed against their capital gain to fund an increasingly indulgent lifestyle. Although the financial crisis didn't take away their jobs, it did end the party. Having their hours cut to save their jobs didn't appeal because the baby boomers worried they would never again return to full-time employment.

In a choice between appealing to a happy voter and appeasing a grumpy one, the standard thinking is to go to where the backlash is. But what happens when the orthodox approach offends young people because they assume, with good reason, that the nation's future belongs to them? On 21 August, Generation Y cast a pro-reform protest vote. They denied Gillard a majority for the same reason that Rudd had lost his job: inaction. I sat in on a Generation Y focus group in the first week of the campaign. I came out thinking Gillard would win comfortably because of the things that were said about Abbott. This was before the leaks, and before the prime minister had repeated her predecessor's error of ducking the issue of climate change. My snapshot of middle Australia comprised eight women in their early to mid-twenties, living in Melbourne's southern suburbs. All were first-home buyers.

The most interesting discussion concerned spending and saving. These women have more cash now than they did as teenagers, but "there is less of it to enjoy." Their definition of thrift is to put money aside for their wedding, or to put off travelling overseas for a year. I asked why they had taken out mortgages so young. The market forced them to. If they were to wait until they were thirty, they would not be able to afford to buy. One had just moved back with her parents and was renting out her home to save money.

The sequence here is mortgage, marriage, then kids. A Coalition pollster would call these women "aspirationals."

Politics didn't come up. The researcher Rebecca Huntley, of Ipsos Mackay, prompted them by asking for thoughts on the election.

"I don't like Tony Abbott's budgie smugglers," one said. "He creeps me out. He looks really creepy," another said.

"I saw a black and white photo of him the other day and ... he looked like a criminal."

"Dodgy."

"Some of the things he says are so uneducated."

They described Gillard as thorough and composed. She was Julia to them.

"She thinks before she speaks."

They still liked Kevin Rudd, the "cool geek," even though he had gone. "He gave us lots of money."

Asked what they did with their stimulus payments, each reply was punctuated with a giggle.

"Shopping."

"Shopping."

"Paid off the credit card and then shopped again."

"Went to Sydney."

On 21 August, the safe Labor seat of Isaacs where the focus group was held saw the Greens' primary vote climb by 4.7 per cent to 10.9 per cent. The swing was at the expense of the Liberal Party, whose primary vote slumped by 4 per cent to 34.5 per cent.

If the Liberals are on the nose in Melbourne's mortgage belt, then Labor's identity crisis could extend to the suburbs in a term or two. Counter-intuitive though this might seem, both sides understand the dynamic. Labor's trouble with the Greens begins with a collapse in the conservative vote. This brings the Greens to within reach of second place, and the opportunity to overtake Labor on preferences.

I know, I know, the two-party system has had more premature death notices than recorded music. Remember the Australian Democrats? In 1990, they secured a primary vote of 11.3 per cent in the lower house, only to see it crash to 3.8 per cent at the following election. Or Pauline Hanson's One Nation? In 1998, they were the first pick of 8.4 per cent of the electorate, but only 4.3 per cent at the next poll.

The Greens' 2010 primary vote of 11.8 per cent could easily recede to single-digits if some routine calamity drives the young back into the arms of Labor or the Coalition. But this is easier said than done while the economy remains strong. Privately, the main parties concede that the Greens represent a structural risk to their respective bases because they have so many young people already on board. If they aren't thinking Labor or Coalition in their twenties and thirties, what would make them change in middle age?

The previous outbreaks against the main parties were driven by outsiders and took place in the context of economic hardship. At its peak, One Nation attracted the support of 16 per cent of men aged fifty-plus, and 12 per cent of those aged 35–49, but their following was in single digits across all other groups. By contrast, the Greens are in double digits across all groups except men aged fifty-plus. They are a pink-and white-collar movement.

The Greens pose an institutional as well as electoral threat to Labor because they appeal to that part of the base that provides parliamentary talent: the professionals. The CV of Adam Bandt, federal member for the seat of Melbourne, mirrors Julia Gillard's. Student politics, then a career in law as a partner at Slater and Gordon. A generation ago Bandt would have joined the party of Whitlam, Hawke and Keating.

To draw a historical analogy, the urban Greens might be to the twenty-first century what the old Country Party was to the 1950s and '60s when the bush still had financial power. The Greens appeal to Generation Y in particular because the party oozes idealism. Bob Brown has become the new Kevin07, the cheery nerd who would liberate us from the lowest-common-denominator politics of the Howard years. Now Labor knows what the Coalition felt like when Rudd first became leader.

The pollster Tony Mitchelmore says the danger for the main parties is that their core voters are just as disillusioned as those who have already taken a leap of faith to go with the Greens.

"What I'm getting in focus groups from people who didn't reach the tipping point is the same attitude, the same frustration, the same description of the behaviour they are sick of as those who have already switched to the Greens," Mitchelmore says. "Ask them to describe the typical politicians; they say they are frauds, they are not genuine, they are not authentic, they are predictably adversarial, they believe in nothing."

The acceleration in the Greens vote is being driven more by instinct than specific issues:

> It goes across a range. At one end it is almost apathy: "What have I got to lose?", "I've tried the other two, they are just going to be more of the same, so why don't I try these other guys?" At the other end of it, there is a bit of an antidote: "At least they stand for something and they have the courage of their convictions." These voters can name the environment as something that they definitely stand for. And further along the spectrum there are the voters who identify

> with the more left values of the Greens and are able to talk about human rights, refugees.

In her post-election analysis, Rebecca Huntley found that voters were frustrated, cynical or angry:

> They have serious problems with the two-party system – specifically the perceived lack of difference between the two major parties – and the apparent inability of our political leaders to think and act long term for the benefit of the nation. They often express their dissatisfaction with the quality of media commentary on politics as well.

There is a telling measure of disenchantment at the ballot box: the combined major-party vote. In the seventeen federal elections held between 1949 and 1987, Labor and the Coalition claimed more than 90 per cent of the first-preference votes between them in all but two of those contests. (The exceptions were 1958 and 1977, the respective debuts of the Democratic Labor Party and the Australian Democrats.)

In the eight federal elections between 1990 and 2010, only one result came close to the 90 per cent benchmark: 1993. Ring any bells? That was Australia's last genuine battle of policies and values, between Paul Keating and John Hewson.

Given that between 15 and 20 per cent of Australians have been voting none of the above for the best part of two decades, the only surprise is that it took so long to hang the parliament.

***

If only Labor and the Coalition could reconnect with their former reformist selves of the 1980s and '90s, when difficult decisions were taken, from the float of the dollar to native title, from tariff cuts to tough gun laws. If they stood for something, there'd be no need for younger voters to project onto the next cleanskin.

Sadly, there are numerous obstacles to this outcome, obvious though its virtues may be. The information revolution and the greying of the population have combined to place a handbrake on reform. As we have seen, the accelerated media cycle makes it almost impossible for leaders to persuade voters to accept decisions in the national interest if someone says no. More than half the electorate wants to impose a price on carbon pollution, but support for action is less overwhelming once pollsters start testing how much people are prepared to pay out of their own pockets. The older the voter, the greater the resistance. And herein lies the rub. Voters aged fifty-plus are fast approaching the point when they will account for half of the electorate. They were 43.9 per cent of all voters in 2007, and 46.1 per cent in 2010. Julia and Tony, meet the baby boomers, the spoilt generation that we can no longer afford to indulge.

Labor was always going to go backwards if it couldn't increase its support within the grey belt. That opportunity passed, paradoxically, with the formal escape from the global financial crisis in early 2009. Nothing the Rudd and Gillard governments offered could compensate for the destruction of retiree nest eggs. Superannuation funds had boasted double-digit returns in the final four years of the Howard government. This wasn't the Coalition's doing, any more than the subsequent falls of 8.1 per cent in 2007–08 and 11.7 per cent in 2008–09 were Labor's fault. But the financial crisis had the same effect on older people that WorkChoices had on the youth belt and working families in 2007: it made them feel poorer at a time of near-full employment.

Tony Abbott sought power on behalf of the grey belt. Stop the boats and the great big new taxes, he said. These are the empty placards of an anti-reform protest party, not the manifesto of an alternative government. But the slogans made more sense to older voters than Julia Gillard's hesitant call to move forward made to the young. Abbott played the generation gridlock card and it almost worked.

The electoral pendulum is telling the Coalition to stick to its oldies base and leave Labor to its existential crisis on the left. But this would be the right's version of power without purpose, because any party that seeks its governing mandate from those at or nearing retirement will have a vested interest in stasis.

Don't underestimate the ability of the grey belt to thwart reform in the future, and to create a generational competition that drives even more young voters away from the main parties and to the Greens.

The needs of the baby boomers collide with those of Generation Y across every conceivable policy challenge facing Australia. Restore the nation's spending on education to international standards? Not if it means baby boomers have to supply some of the spending cuts to make way for a knowledge nation. Make housing more affordable? Not if it means baby boomers lose their capital gain. Use a market-based mechanism to handle climate change? Not if it means baby boomers can't be made better off in the transition.

***

Apart from young and old, there is one other key fault-line for the nation. Travel down the east coast of Australia and Labor's vote after the distribution of preferences increased by about 5 percentage points with each crossing of the border. From 45 per cent in Queensland, to 49 per cent in New South Wales, to 55 per cent in Victoria and, over the Bass Strait, 60 per cent in Tasmania. The schism between Queensland and Victoria is echoed between the blue state of Western Australia (Labor's weakest, on 44 per cent) and the red state of South Australia (53 per cent). Mining states versus manufacturing states; conservative states versus progressive states.

In political and social terms, Victoria is Venus, Queensland is Mars. Victoria is the state the rest of Australia imagines itself to be – pro-market and pro-immigration. Queensland is the least urbanised state in the nation, and its capital, Brisbane, has the lowest proportion of overseas-born residents of the big four Australian cities. It has jumped from outpost to major state over the past two decades, but it has yet to lose its sense of otherness in its cultural argument with the rest of the nation.

Queensland has traditionally swung hard against Labor governments, leaving Paul Keating with just two seats in 1996 and Gough Whitlam only one in 1975. But it rarely goes against an incumbent when the rest of the nation isn't in a mood for retribution. The 2010 election was the first since 1984 when the Sunshine State backed the wrong side by giving a majority of seats to the Opposition.

To see the fractures more clearly, imagine the federal parliament as three zones of roughly equal size. The southern, or progressive, states of Victoria, South Australia, Tasmania and the ACT hold 55 seats. The mining, or conservative, states of Queensland, Western Australia and the Northern Territory have 47 seats. Sitting between the two is the dead state of New South Wales, with 48 seats.

In net terms, the southern states swung two seats to the left – 36 out of 55. New South Wales moved four seats to the right, but Labor still held the majority –

26 out of 48, plus the two rural independents it picked up afterward. The wipe-out occurred in the mining states, where Labor lost half its seats, leaving it with a miserable 12 out of 47.

Labor was on the nose in the north and the west because people felt worse off, notwithstanding Australia's artful dodge of the global recession. The crowding out associated with a resources boom affected every aspect of society, business and government in the mining states.

For the locals, cost of living pressures are exploding. For the new arrivals from interstate, home ownership is out of reach because of high prices and shortages. There are 56,000 more willing buyers than there are available houses and units in Queensland, while the supply gap in Western Australia is 30,000. And for Labor, years of cutting corners on infrastructure, health and education at the state level rebounded against a first-term federal government.

The unease in Queensland dates back to the introduction of WorkChoices in 2006. Voters began blaming John Howard for everything, including the water shortages that were a state responsibility. Sure, Queenslanders still had jobs. But the state was at near-full employment when it sacked the Coalition government in 2007.

"It's getting really hard to live in Queensland," was how Labor's post-election analysis put it.

The affairs of the states are fast becoming the most pressing concern of federal government. State Labor is exhausted in New South Wales, where it has held power for twenty-seven of the last thirty-four years. Labor's dismissal is expected next March. In Queensland, Labor has ruled for all but three of the last twenty-one years, and its chances of earning another term in 2012 are slim. These two states have the nation's least efficient energy markets, so their households will wear the sharpest spikes in prices under an emissions trading scheme or a carbon tax. But there is no point in Gillard agonising over this transaction, because federal Labor will lose even more votes to the Greens if it continues to prevaricate on climate change. New South Wales and Queensland also have the greatest need for new infrastructure spending. Without the revenue that flows from a mining tax, Gillard can't help to meet those demands.

Gillard has no choice, really, but to pursue reform, even if it means federal Labor suffers at the next election. The alternative is another term of do-nothing government, which, as 21 August demonstrated, isn't smart politics anyway.

The false economy of poll-driven government should be apparent to both sides by now. Labor ceases to be a viable stand-alone party if it cedes a generation of voters, and party members, to the Greens. For the Coalition, the demographic time bomb is ticking just as loudly. It has even less support among young voters than Labor and can't claim a positive mandate while it presents itself as a protest party for the grey belt alone.

Rudd, Gillard and Abbott sought power in 2010 on the same dangerous premise, that no sacrifice is required to secure our future. Government on this basis is never worth it because the promise of painless change can never be kept. The voters knew it, which is why they spared themselves the inevitable let-down by hanging the parliament.

The Power of No

Before the news and polling cycles accelerated, leaders assumed that the electorate understood reform was a long game. Not anymore. The digital age has shrunk the public attention span and lured government into making each thing it says *appear* to be a big idea.

While impatience remains the dominant instinct in politics, and in our wider culture, both sides will err on the side of hyperbole. The best ever, no, the worst in history.

And still they wonder why the backlash comes when delivery doesn't meet expectation. We saved you from recession. No, you set my roof on fire. Hang on, you let that dodgy installer into your house. It's a circular conversation that government can only break if it starts playing its role again by telling voters what is and isn't possible.

Australia has acquired a form of policy paralysis by over-analysis. The problem isn't the quality of the advice, because there is more of it than ever before if leaders know where to look. The system is broken because the prosperity generation of politicians has been too willing to junk good policy when the pollster says so.

If too much information can make you stupid, then we have seen it in the way our leaders have tried to be simultaneously expert, celebrity, philosopher and number-cruncher. Labor gave us know-it-alls in Mark Latham and Kevin Rudd. The Liberal Party's version was Malcolm Turnbull. If a policy adviser has managed to convince any of the above to change their mind without resorting to a poll, I'd like to dedicate this essay to them.

Julia Gillard's instincts are to under-promise and over-deliver. On the other hand, what makes Julia so much more normal than Mark, Kevin, Malcolm and Tony might be the very thing that prevents her from being a successful prime minister: she doesn't have the touch of madness that allows a leader to inspire.

Gillard says Australia gave Labor a mixed report card for its first term:

> I think the electorate did give us a tick for the response to the global financial crisis. They did realise that the government action made a difference. But people were also sending us a series of concerns about implementation. I think there was well and truly a message about, on the one hand urban congestion, on the other hand border protection, and obviously it was in the political interests of the Opposition to conflate these concepts in people's minds. And I think on climate change there was a message too. They were saying to us they weren't sure of what the message was.

Gillard concedes that governments have yet to work out how to run meaningful debates in the digital age. Political parties have adapted new technologies for electioneering, and she cites Barack Obama's presidential campaign of 2008 as the benchmark. But this method doesn't translate to governing: "The conducting of conversations from government is different to campaign communications and I don't think the way of having a national conversation has changed yet."

The 24-hour news cycle traps governments into "conversations that are thin, but not deep," she says.

> Something that was a blockbuster at 10a.m. when it's announced has been tweeted about by 10.05, has been blogged about by 10.30. Then on 24-hour TV journalists have taken to interviewing journalists about what it may or may not mean and what politicians may or may not have been thinking when they announced it. And by midday someone will be ringing my press office saying, "Have you got a story for me?" That's the nature of the cycle and I think we are still adapting to that change. One of the things I'm trying to signal by saying my focus isn't going to be the six o'clock news is to try and work through how we sustain deep conversations rather than thin conversations in this environment.

She isn't saying less is more, but that saying the same thing more often, and in different ways, is what government should be aiming for:

> I think part of the lesson for government is if you are going to sustain deep conversations then you need to be very clear about your priorities and pick what you are investing in in terms of those conversations. You won't be able to have it across this huge broad range of fronts.

The logic of this observation is that Gillard will need to risk ignoring the media when she has nothing new to say, or when the citizenry's attention is distracted by, say, another round of kiss-and-tell stories about Tiger Woods.

Gillard has a radical thought about the hung parliament. She says it will re-earth politicians and the media by making both concentrate on the legislative process. It's an optimistic view that assumes the distinctiveness of minority government will prompt journalists to reconsider how they report politics.

She had already intended to change the way government operated, to give the caucus a greater say in the formulation of legislation. Gone is Rudd's gang of four, of which she was a member:

> Whether or not we'd had the hung parliament, it was my intention to have a different way of working in caucus so people are involved in the ideas-generation stage, so they can put things on

> the table rather than [cabinet saying], "Here's a fully formed idea, yes or no," and then the parliamentary process is, "Here's the fully formed idea, are you for it or against it?" This is going to be a different way of working for us internally, for us as a parliament, and I think in terms of sustaining national conversations that will actually help.

But there are also some disturbing aspects to the hung parliament that suggest not much will be achieved. A hung parliament contains a hint of politics the American way, where power is bought one contrary MP at a time. The independents mostly played it straight in the negotiations to form minority government, and they made the nation feel a little better about itself as it watched the main parties crawl. The New South Wales rural independents, Tony Windsor and Rob Oakeshott, and the Tasmanian independent, Andrew Wilkie, didn't go to the highest bidder, because Tony Abbott offered them much more money. But they did extract cash for their causes. Legislation on the same terms would be messy at best, and damaging to the nation at worst.

***

Logic suggests that the revival of policy-driven government should follow the exhaustion of the poll-driven alternative. For Labor, the example of Rudd and the reality of a hung parliament ought to loosen the grip of the polling and media cycles on its collective psyche. A good poll or two from now on can't be taken seriously because Rudd had them for two years before losing his job. Equally, a bad poll or two can't make the government any more vulnerable, because it has already ceded its majority.

An optimist would see Gillard's modest personal approval rating, and Labor's continued weak primary vote, as a blessing. With no lead to protect, she can only rebuild Labor's standing through achievement, one negotiated piece of legislation at a time. Yet government is not the ideal place from which to remake a political party. Labor's greatest periods of renewal came in Opposition after heavy defeats. Gough Whitlam took the Labor leadership after the 1966 election thrashing and modernised the party's social program within two terms. Bill Hayden took another two terms to restore Labor's economic credibility after the profligacy of the Whitlam government. Hayden is the often forgotten co-author of the Hawke–Keating reforms. He was the first Labor leader to embrace the market and the now outdated notion that new spending has to be paid for by cuts elsewhere or through increased taxation. Gillard needs to channel both Whitlam and Hayden if her minority government is to effect change.

Any reform that Gillard secures will no doubt have poll-watchers obsessing again as they run a line through the public response. Here's a quick guide to reading these things: the first poll is meaningless because it usually favours the decision-maker. Paul Keating received a healthy bounce in his personal rating after the *Mabo* legislation was passed in December 1993; John Howard enjoyed a similar improvement after he struck his GST deal with the Australian Democrats in May 1999. The voters pay on results, but they are liable to ask for their money back if the implementation goes awry. The harder task for any government is to keep the conversation going.

Gillard's checklist for reform begins with an issue where very few Labor seats are directly at risk: the Murray–Darling basin. Water is an issue that both sides supposedly agree on, and Labor will rely on Howard-government legislation for its proposed buy-back of irrigation licences to restore flows to the river system. The premise of water reform is that too many licences were issued by state governments in the past, compromising the very viability of the Murray–Darling. This process will be difficult because country towns that rely on irrigation will have to find new sources of income. Unlike most reforms, though, water is one area where the losers can be compensated on generous terms, at the expense of the general taxpayer. If the government purchases water on behalf of the environment, the farmers concerned receive a cash buffer that they can use either to diversify their crop or to seek work in another field. Manufacturing workers did not enjoy the same luxury when the tariff wall came down in the

1980s and '90s. They bore the cost of a reform that benefited the wider community.

The environment was Labor's home turf until it botched the emissions trading scheme. The people were prepared to pay, but Rudd and then Gillard hesitated. Yet Labor had reason to believe that sacrifice for the environment had become a popular cause because when state governments tested support for water restrictions, they found, to their surprise, that the public was happy to contribute. One Labor premier told me that he couldn't ease the restrictions for fear of a voter backlash.

The independents want to act as Labor's conscience, nudging Gillard and her ministers towards reforms that were deemed too hard in the first term. There seems to be a commonality of interests here because the prime minister will want to secure her base in the southern states, and recapture some of the Labor defectors who went to the Greens, by legislating for a mining tax and a price on carbon pollution.

But these are the two agendas that helped turn Queensland against Labor. The Opposition leader will be under pressure to continue to obstruct both if he wants to keep the mining states in the Coalition camp. The tightness of the numbers gives Abbott the opportunity to play the game hard, Malcolm Fraser-style. He might recall that the electorate didn't punish the conservatives for the crisis of 1975, even though it was their manipulation of the Senate casual vacancy process that allowed them to defer supply to the Whitlam government – the precondition for Labor's dismissal.

Australia's crisis of governance is part of a global pattern. Great Britain has a hung parliament, and the United States has been testing new forms of gridlock. Barack Obama has some big reforms to his name, most notably on health care, but he is cursed with the same decline in popularity as the do-nothing Rudd and Gillard governments.

The president blames himself for assuming that reform would sell itself. "Given how much stuff was coming at us, we probably spent much more time trying to get the policy right than trying to get the politics right," he told the *New York Times* in an interview published in October 2010.

> There is probably a perverse pride in my administration – and I take responsibility for this; this was blowing from the top – that we were going to do the right thing, even if short-term it was unpopular. And I think anybody who's occupied this office has to remember that success is determined by an intersection in policy and politics and that you can't be neglecting of marketing and PR and public opinion.

Damned if you reform, and damned if you don't.

Obama carries the handicap of an unemployment rate that is double ours. Yet his experience is nonetheless familiar. Obama's approval rating displayed a Rudd-like quality in the early stages. In fact, his numbers in the first 100 days of his presidency were the strongest in a generation – better than those of Ronald Reagan, the two George Bushes and Bill Clinton at the same stage. Then came the steady slide from a percentage figure in the high 60s to the low 40s. Obama's trajectory after almost two years in office is identical to that of Reagan, who also inherited an economy in deep recession.

While Australians may never entertain the extremes of the American psyche of god, guns and greed, our politicians do adopt the American habits of government and Opposition. Rudd wanted to be Obama, the messiah, and Tony Abbott has taken a leaf from the book of Sarah Palin, the snark in exile. The Opposition leader looked to the United States and saw that the Republicans could rough up a popular Democrat president who had control of both houses of congress simply by saying "No."

Obama admits that he underestimated the ability of the Republicans to slow down the legislative process at his expense. In September he told *Rolling Stone* magazine:

> Even if you eventually got something done, it would take so long and it would be so contentious, that it sent the message to the public that "Gosh, Obama said he was going to come in

> and change Washington, and it's exactly the same, it's more contentious than ever."
>
> Everything just seems to drag on – even what should be routine activities, like appointments, aren't happening. So it created an atmosphere in which a public that is already very sceptical of government, but was maybe feeling hopeful right after my election, felt deflated and sort of felt "We're just seeing more of the same."

The global financial crisis has been a killer of incumbents, flipping the mood that existed immediately after the 11 September 2001 terrorist attacks when almost every government around the world recorded swings to it.

The financial crisis has pitted young against old, and it has compounded the two trends that have undermined government. The long story is the end of the Cold War, which has forced the major parties to exaggerate the ideological differences that remain between them – a squabble that turns off voters. The more recent catalyst is the internet. Australia has not been immune from these forces, despite its two-decades-long boom.

Journalists fear their loss of authority in the digital age will undermine their ability to hold government to account. Yet government has much more to worry about because the internet has empowered vested interests, and Oppositions, in a way that can effectively cancel an election result within weeks of the final ballot being counted. Obama used the internet to market his genius in 2008. But his strategic insight was applied against him in office because his opponents uncovered the veto of white noise. They could yell and blame him for the ruckus, because he was the fancy-pants who had promised change. The Coalition hit on the same idea late in Rudd's first term, but the results were just as spectacular. Rudd had a meltdown, and Gillard almost went the same way.

The fact that a prosperous Australia suffers a version of the politics that cripples a recessed United States suggests the explanation is structural, not cyclical. Western democracies, I fear, are fast approaching the point where they become ungovernable because anyone can say "No."

Government is weaker today because the public it serves is quicker to anger, and because the Opposition has realised the safest way back to power is opposition, not policy renewal. No mandate need be respected because the Opposition can trust the media to set impossible standards for governments to meet.

The American polls show that what politics has lost over the past generation is respect. The last US president who appealed to both sides of politics was Reagan. Every president since then has drawn the bulk of his approval rating from his party's supporters only – the other side marked him so low you could swear they were biased. This is their version of Australia's large none-of-the-above primary vote since 1990. We share a political culture that is both polarised and disengaged.

Reagan ruled in the 1980s, when Bob Hawke and Paul Keating were at the peak of their reformist powers. The Liberals back then offered Labor bipartisanship on the two most crucial elements of the reform push: the floating of the dollar and the removal of tariff protection. The Liberals did oppose Medicare, the assets test for the age pension, the capital-gains tax and, later, universal superannuation. But they gave Labor respect where it mattered.

The emissions trading scheme should have marked a return to form for our system. On any fair reading of the numbers in the parliament, two-thirds of all MPs – that is, most on the Labor side, the Greens and up to half the Coalition – supported action on climate change. Yet minority interests prevailed. Polluters extracted concessions that made the budget worse off, before the half of the Opposition who didn't believe in climate change scuttled the compromised legislation. If Australia can't secure reform where majority support already exists, then it has taken the first step on the road back to mediocrity.

What makes me pessimistic about the nation's politics now is the character of many of the people in it. The crew that delivered us such a silly campaign have to behave like adults to make the hung parliament work.

They will need to overcome a generational instinct for instant gratification.

Before they can re-educate the electorate, they must first re-train themselves.

Sources

BALANCING ACT

"The economy was the primary reason": Malcolm Turnbull, doorstop interview, Canberra, 14 September 2015.

"It was on Abbott's watch": International Monetary Fund, Australia, IMF Country Report No. 15/274, September 2015.

"but this time it didn't": Australia's unemployment rate was 5.6 per cent when the Abbott government came to power in September 2013, 1.7 percentage points below the US unemployment rate of 7.3 per cent. A year later, the lines had crossed, and by September 2015, when Tony Abbott was removed as prime minister, Australia's unemployment rate was 6.1 per cent compared to the US 5.1 per cent. For the Australian data, see: Australian Bureau of Statistics, *Labour Force, Australia,* cat. no. 6202.0, ABS, Canberra, December 2015, table 1. For the US data, see United States Department of Labor, Bureau of Labor Statistics, http://data.bls.gov/timeseries/LNS 14000000.

"The media post-mortems": Peter Hartcher, "Shirtfronted: The story of the Abbott government," *Sydney Morning Herald,* 29 November – 3 December

2015, www.smh.com.au/interactive/2015/Shirtfronted/.

"Mr Speaker, the Abbott government": Joe Hockey's valedictory speech, *Hansard,* 21 October 2015, p.11947.

"We need to restore": Turnbull, 14 September 2015.

"the first Labor leader to win office when the economy was strong": Gough Whitlam, by contrast, took power in December 1972, following a prolonged slowdown in the economy. GDP had contracted in three of the previous four quarters - a recession by any definition. See Australian Bureau of Statistics, *Australian National Accounts: National Income, Expenditure and Product,* cat. no. 5206.0, ABS, Canberra, September 2015, table 2.

"smallest pay rise since the wages system was deregulated": "The through the year rise for the private sector was the smallest rate of wages growth recorded since the start of the series." Australian Bureau of Statistics, *Wage Price Index, Australia,* cat. no. 6345.0, ABS, Canberra, September 2015.

"The unexpected story": Calculations for male and female employment by industry, Australian Bureau of Statistics, *Labour Force, Australia, Detailed, Quarterly,* cat. no. 6291.0.55.003, Canberra, ABS, November 2015, tables 04 and 06.

"Household debt": Reserve Bank of Australia, *Statistical Tables,* www.rba.gov.au/statistics/tables/, table E2, column D.

"Public investment fell": Calculations from ABS, cat. no. 5206.0, table 3.

"Ken Henry explains": Interview with author for the ABC television series *Making Australia Great: Inside Our Longest Boom.* Comments were not broadcast on the show.

"The IMF chided the Abbott government": IMF, *Australia.*

"Joel Deane chronicled the mistakes": Joel Deane, *Catch and Kill: The Politics of Power,* University of Queensland Press, 2015, pp.176–8.

"We are one of just three developed nations": Calculations for employment rates made from OECD, *Short-Term Labour Market Statistics,* http://stats.oecd.org/Index.aspx?DataSetCode=STLABOUR, data extracted on 30 October 2015, 06:33 UTC (GMT) from OECD. Stat.

"In the full employment 1960s": ABS, cat. no. 5206.0, table 24.

"Ken Henry says": Interview with author for *Making Australia Great: Inside Our Longest Boom.* Part of this section of the interview was broadcast in the third episode.

"The dog days for New South Wales": Data for state growth taken from Australian Bureau of Statistics, *Australian National Accounts: State Accounts, 2014–15,* cat. no. 5220.0, ABS, Canberra, 20 November 2015, table 1.

"39 per cent of Sydney's population are overseas-born": Migration statistics taken from Australian Bureau of Statistics, *Australian Social Trends, 2014,* cat. no. 4102.0, ABS, Canberra, 18 March 2014; and from author's calculations based on raw tables from the 2011 census supplied to him by the ABS in August 2012.

"Those that score best": The Economist Intelligence Unit, *A Summary of the Liveability Ranking and Overview,* August 2014.

"we had something the Chinese wanted": Department of Foreign Affairs and Trade, *Australia's Trade at a Glance,* summary of Australia's trade with China, http://dfat.gov.au/trade/resources/trade-at-a-glance/Pages/default.aspx; US trade with China: United States Census Bureau, *Trade in Goods with China,* www.census.gov/foreign-trade/balance/c5700.html. Note the figures quoted are in Australian and US dollars respectively. Comparison is based on trade in goods only.

"Paul Volcker": Interview with author for *Making Australia Great: Inside Our Longest Boom.* Comments were not broadcast on the show.

"The total tax take": Calculations taken from Australian Government, *Budget 2014–15,* supplementary table 2.

"By 2005–06, it would be $3.8 billion": George Megalogenis, "Tax-as-you-earn workers stung by $3.8bn bracket creep," *Weekend Australian,* 21 February 2004, p.1.

"between $20 billion and $31.5 billion": Ben Phillips and Amar Vohra, "Bracket creep a big factor in Australian living standards," *SAS-Natsem Report,* NATSEM, 18 December 2015.

"If you knew for a fact": Ken Henry, interview with author for *Making Australia Great: Inside Our Longest Boom.* Comments were not broadcast on the show.

"the tax cuts made Australia less fair": Nicolas Herault and Fransisco Azpitarte, "Understanding changes in the distribution and redistribution of income: A unifying decomposition framework," *Review of Income and Wealth,* 12 December 2014.

"John Howard remains unrepentant": Interview with author for *Making Australia Great: Inside Our Longest*

Boom. Part of this section of the interview was broadcast in the third episode.

"They saw him being opportunistic": Mark Textor, interview with author for *Making Australia Great: Inside Our Longest Boom.* Comments were not broadcast on the show.

"The most telling article": Dennis Atkins, "No tax unstudied as Malcolm Turnbull's cabinet creates mud map for reform," *Courier-Mail,* 14 November 2015.

"I thought we were very close": Ian Macfarlane, interview with author for *Making Australia Great, Inside Our Longest Boom.* This is an edited version of comments broadcast in the second episode.

"Sydney house prices": Australian Bureau of Statistics, *Residential Property Price Indexes: Eight Capital Cities,* cat. no. 6416.0, ABS, Canberra, September 2015, tables 2 and 3.

"An unintended benefit": Reserve Bank of Australia, *Monetary Policy,* www.rba.gov.au/monetary-policy/ – details of Australian official interest rates are summarised under "interest rate decisions." For US and other international official interest rates, see RBA, Statistical Tables, table F13.

"The landlord class": Calculations from Australian Taxation Office, *Taxation Statistics 2012–13,* table 1.

"does that really matter?": Ken Henry, interview with author for *Making Australia Great: Inside Our Longest Boom.* Comments were not broadcast on the show.

"John Quiggin pointed out": John Quiggin, "How New Zealand Fell Further Behind," *Inside Story* (online), 11 November 2015.

"Mark Textor says voters have grasped": Interview with author for *Making Australia Great: Inside Our Longest Boom.* Comments were not broadcast on the show.

"It was a harbinger": Before 2007, the lowest primary vote for an incoming Labor government was Jim Scullin's 48.8 per cent in 1929. Kevin Rudd's entry vote was 43.5 per cent and his exit vote in 2013 was 33.4 per cent. The evidence at state level is that the next federal Labor government may return to office with a primary vote below 40 per cent. It has already done this twice in Queensland, in 1988 and 2015, and once each in Western Australia (2001), South Australia (2002) and Victoria (2014). Note that Julia Gillard won minority government in 2010 with a primary vote of 38 per cent, which was 0.8 per cent lower than the primary vote Paul Keating was defeated with in 1996.

"The shifts in global economic power": Calculations from the International Monetary Fund, *World Economic*

Outlook Database, October 2015, www.imf.org/external/pubs/ft/weo/2015/02/weodata/weoselgr.aspx.

"A troubling spike in deaths": Anne Case and Angus Deaton, "Rising morbidity and mortality in midlife among white non-Hispanic Americans in the 21st century," *Proceedings of the National Academy of Sciences of the United States of America,* vol. 112, no. 49, 17 September 2015.

"Professor Bob Gregory has found": Tables supplied by Professor Gregory, which he used for his speech "The Amazing Decade: The Million People Surprise," Social and Economic Outlook Conference, Melbourne, 5 November 2015.

"'You cannot turn your back on your party base'": James Law, "Knives out for Turnbull after election 'disaster,'" news.com.au, 4 July 2016, www.news.com.au/national/federal-election/knives-out-for-turnbull-after-electiondisaster/news-story/9020ba449c110e57cbc9ebf76edf505e.

"Textor had said that far right-wing websites don't matter": Tim Blair, "Clarification," *The Daily Telegraph,* 28 September 2015, www.dailytelegraph.com.au/blogs/tim-blair/clarification/news-story/86252390667f48c8cdc499f6b51247dc.

"Before he became prime minister": Turnbull repeatedly argued that a free vote on same-sex marriage was consistent with Liberal Party traditions. But you can see the switch from principle to pragmatism in the blog he wrote on 16 August 2015, and the update eleven days later: www.malcolmturnbull.com.au/media/blog-ssm. The switch on the Racial Discrimination Act is more subtle. As recently as August 2016, he was saying: "The Government has no plans to change 18C, we have other, much more pressing priorities to address and they include big economic reforms." Jane Norman, "Turnbull says Government has no plans to change 18c as backbench pushes for race hate law changes," ABC News, 31 August 2016, www.abc.net.au/news/2016-08-31/turnbull-says-government-has-no-plans-to-change-18c-race-laws/7801254. By November, he was entertaining a review: see Jane Norman, "18C: Malcolm Turnbull refuses to rule out freedom of speech inquiry as backbench pressure grows," ABC News, 4 November 2016, www.abc.net.au/news/2016-11-04/turnbull-wont-block-inquiry-into-freedom-of-speech/7996366.

"Western Australia had closed the last decade": www.aph.gov.au/About_Parliament/Parliamentary_Departments/Parliamentary_Budget_Office/Reports/Research_reports/Report_032016. See Data: "Table 2: General government data by level of government as at 2016-17 budgets (as published)", line 37.

TRIVIAL PURSUIT

"Between 1940 and 1987, Labor recorded": Here are Labor's primary votes each time it took government from Opposition since World War II:

1972 49.6 per cent
1983 49.5 per cent
2007 43.38 per cent

And the primaries since 1990:

1990 39.4 per cent
1993 44.9 per cent
1996 38.8 per cent
1998 40.1 per cent
2001 37.8 per cent
2004 37.6 per cent
2007 43.38 per cent
2010 37.99 per cent

"press secretary David Luff revealed": David Luff, "PM needs something to numb his pain," *The Sunday Telegraph,* 1 June 2008.

"When I fought the 1997 election": Tony Blair's speech was given on 12 June 2007, fifteen days before he resigned as prime minister. See http://news.bbc.co.uk/2/hi/uk_news/politics/6744581.stm.

"Menzies and Murdoch engaged in an angry exchange": The account of the Menzies–Murdoch feud is sourced to Bridget Griffen-Foley's *Party Games: Australian Politicians and the Media from War to Dismissal,* Text, Melbourne, 2003, pp.24–28. Griffen-Foley says that "there is no evidence to suggest that he [Sir Keith Murdoch] had deliberately solicited a poll to destabilise Menzies' leadership." I think a reverse burden of proof should apply in these cases: a politician should be assumed to be paranoid unless he can prove otherwise.

"If it serves to tell the politician": *New York Times Magazine,* 28 November 1948.

"The early polls also showed": Gallup poll taken on 30 March 1951.

"[His] first memory is of the steam train": Michael Duffy, *Latham and Abbott: The Lives and Rivalry of the Two Finest Politicians of Their Generation,* Random House, Milson's Point NSW, 2004, p.10.

"Abbott gave a speech calling for tolerance": The Opposition leader gave his Big Australia speech on 22 January 2010 in Melbourne. See www.tonyabbott.com.au/latestnews/speeches/tabid/88/articletype/articleview/articleid/7228/address-to-the-australia-day-council-victoria-australia-day-dinner-melbourne.aspx.

"Like two old bulls who didn't know when to stop charging": The Hawke–Keating section is adapted from my article "Paul Keating unleashes on Bob Hawke: I carried you through years of 'malaise,'" *The Australian,* 15 July 2010.

"But only after saying he wouldn't compromise": John Howard made the comment on 19 February 2001.

"Ross Garnaut used a lecture": "Climate Change, China Booms and Australia's Governance Struggle in a Changing World," 2010 Hamer Oration, University of Melbourne and Hamer Family Fund, 5 August 2010.

"Treasury had sharp words for both sides": The Blue Book was released by Shadow Treasurer Joe Hockey. The incoming brief for the Labor government, the Red Book, can be found at www.treasury.gov.au/contentitem.asp?ContentID=1875&NavID=007.

"telling the pollsters they preferred increased spending to tax cuts": See Juliet Clark and Ian McAllister, *Trends in Australian Political Opinion: Results from the Australian Election Study 1987–2007,* p. 29, available at http://assda.anu.edu.au/aestrends.pdf; and Richard Grant, *Less Tax or More Social Spending: Twenty Years of Opinion Polling, Information and Research Services,* Parliamentary Library, Department of Parliamentary Services, 2004, available at www.aph.gov.au/library/pubs/rp/2003-04/04rp13.pdf.

"Tom Albanese, went on Sydney talkback radio": 2GB, 3 June 2010. Media Monitors transcript.

"In his book on the Chinese Community Party": Richard McGregor, *The Party: The Secret World of China's Communist Rulers,* Harper Collins, New York, 2010, p.61.

"state income during the global financial crisis": Figures taken from the Australian Bureau of Statistics report 5220.0, *Australian National Accounts: State Accounts,* 2008-09.

"For the first time in our history": I've taken Brian Loughnane's speech from Malcolm Farnsworth's blog, AustralianPolitics.com, "Liberal Party Director Analyses Election Defeat," 19 December 2007.

"The result, in a nutshell": Newspoll, unpublished demographic breakdown. I've rounded the totals, as these numbers jump around a bit from poll to poll. The 17–19 August results were:

> Men aged 18–34: Labor 29.9 per cent, Coalition 36.6 per cent, Greens 25.5 per cent. Women aged 18–34: Labor 39.3 per cent, Coalition 32.9 per cent, Greens 18.1 per cent.

"I sat in on a Generation Y focus group": focus group conducted as part of the *Ipsos Mackay Report.*

"On 21 August, the safe Labor seat": Election results sourced from the AEC's Virtual Tally Room (http://vtr.aec.gov.au). The final count for Isaacs can be found at http://vtr.aec.gov.au/HouseDivisionFirstPrefs-15508-219.htm.

"At its peak, One Nation": Newspoll, unpublished demographic breakdown for the September quarter, 1998. One Nation's total primary vote among men was 12.2 per cent, but for women it was 7.7 per cent.

"There is a telling measure of disenchantment at the ballot box": Figures taken from the *AEC Electoral Pocketbook,* revised edition, April 2009.

"Superannuation funds had boasted double-digit returns": Figures taken from Table 13, *Annual Superannuation Bulletin,* June 2009. Available at www.apra.gov.au/Statistics/Annual-Superannuation-Publication.cfm.

"one other key fault-line for the nation": Labor's two-party vote for each state, travelling north to south and east to west, to two decimal points:

Queensland 44.86 per cent
New South Wales 48.84 per cent
Victoria 55.31 per cent
Tasmania 60.62 per cent
South Australia 53.18 per cent

Western Australia 43.59 per cent

"For the locals, cost of living pressures are exploding": See Table 4.5 of the National Housing Supply Council's 2010 State of Supply Report, www.nhsc.org.au/state_of_supply/2009_ssr_rpt/SoSR_ch4.htm#ch4_2.

I conducted dozens of interviews before and after the 2010 election. The following are the dates of the interviews that yielded for-the-record quotes. The other politicians, party figures and officials I spoke to will, of course, remain nameless.

The politicians: John Howard, 20 September; Wayne Swan, 22 September; Simon Crean, 23 September; and Julia Gillard, 29 September.

The pollsters: Rod Cameron, founder of ANOP, 15 September; Neil Lawrence, founder of Lawrence Creative Strategy, 18 September; and Tony Mitchelmore, founder of Visibility, 21 September.

Back Cover Material

"Australia is in transition. Saying it is easy. The panic kicks in when we are compelled to describe what the future might look like. There is no complacent middle to aim at. We will either catch the next wave of prosperity, or finally succumb to the Great Recession."

What has gone wrong with our politics? And what does our government need to do so that Australia is not globalisation's next victim? *Balancing Act* is a passionate look at the politics of change and renewal, and a bold call for active government. George Megalogenis argues that both sides of politics are clinging to an old model because it tells them a reassuring story of Australian success. But that model has been exhausted by capitalism's extended crisis and the end of the mining boom. It is time to redraw the line between market and state.

This revised edition of Megalogenis's bestselling Quarterly Essay brings the story up to date through a substantial new essay, and also includes his other acclaimed Quarterly Essay, *Trivial Pursuit: Leadership and the End of the Reform Era.*

GEORGE MEGALOGENIS has thirty years' experience in the media, including over a decade in the federal parliamentary press gallery. His book *The Australian*

Moment won the 2013 Prime Minister's Literary Award for non-fiction and the 2012 Walkley Award for non-fiction, and formed the basis for his ABC TV series *Making Australia Great.* His most recent book is *Australia's Second Chance.*

Made in United States
North Haven, CT
05 November 2026

21766935R00135